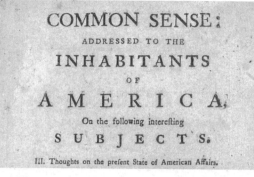

COMMON SENSE:
ADDRESSED TO THE
INHABITANTS
OF
AMERICA,
On the following interesting
SUBJECTS.
III. Thoughts on the present State of American Affairs.

Common Sense in Uncommon Times

SURVIVAL IN A CHANGING WORLD

Brian L. Crissey, Ph.D.
Pamela Meyer Crissey, C.H.

Granite Publishing
PO Box 1429
Columbus, NC 28722

Library of Congress Cataloging-in-Publication Data

Crissey, Brian, 1947-

Common sense in uncommon times: survival in a changing world / Brian L. Crissey, Ph.D., and Pamela M. Crissey, C.H. -- 2 Edition 176 pages cm

Includes bibliographical references and index.

ISBN 978-1-893183-55-1 (pbk. : alk. paper) --
ISBN 978-1-893183-56-8 (ebk.) (print)

1. Survival. 2. Evacuation of civilians. 3. Terrorism. 4. Bioterrorism.

I. Crissey, Pamela 1949-   II. Title.   GF86.M49 2012

613.6'9--dc23

2012045432

Cover Photo: licensed from Corbis Images

Disclaimer: Any medical advice in this book is not a substitute for visiting your health practitioner.

Printed in the United States of America.

Address all inquiries to:

Granite Publishing

P.O. Box 1429

Columbus, NC 28722

http://granitepublishing.us

Dedication

To our children and grandchildren
and the as-yet unborn
who await us
in our sustainable future—
children who are cherished,
with faces not yet familiar,
but whose loving presence
pulls us gently forward,
so they can live.

Acknowledgments

To all those who have touched us
in any way,
at any time,
for their touch molded us
and provided grist for the mill
that ground out this book.

The Cover

This solitary house in Gilchrist, Texas,
survived Hurricane Ike in 2008.
Originally standing 14 feet above the surf,
it is an amazing symbol of
survival through difficult times.
The house could not anticipate the storm,
but it was prepared for it.

The Sandy Face of Change

Harm without malice,
Sandy is like you and me—
With a name, a story and a purpose.

She flattens Jamaican shanties,
Drifting by the foot in Snowshoe,
And flooding tunnels with hot and cold running water.

She rakes corn fields in Iowa,
Making feather dusters of Carolina oaks,
And dropping the flag on those whose expiration date has passed.

She breaches breakwaters,
Moving sandy dunes to let the ocean surge,
And clearing traffic and noise from Times Square.

She closes bridges and freeways,
Turning lights out and phones off,
And making Ground Zero a reflection pool.

She dismisses elections and markets,
Making those with cell-based identities
Wonder who they really are today.

Bigger than Alaska,
She touches everyone,
This storm of the century.

She has a job
And she does it—
She gets our attention.

To those who can hear,
She whispers in the virgin
silence,
"Listen. Observe. Learn."
LOL

I top off the oil in the generator and replace its plug.
I split and stack old solar energy,
Manifest in tree bones.

Not to battle Mother Earth,
Which is foolish,

But as *Common Sense*,
which is wise.

Brian L. Crissey

How To Use This Book

*EVERYTHING YOU NEED TO KNOW,
YOU LEARNED FROM NOAH'S ARK...
KNOWLEDGE AND PREPARATION GIVE YOU CONFIDENCE.*

We do not know when a bomb will detonate, a tsunami will sweep in, or the very earth beneath our feet will quake and topple debris on us. These are unknowns that we live with, so what can we do about them? This book provides you with the methods, resources, and understandings required to gain confidence to handle sudden or impending events with greater ease, which helps dissipate fear. Beyond its role in motivating you to not retouch a hot stove that burned you before, fear is not only unnecessary—it can be dangerous: Fear prevents calm, common-sense thinking.

Since the first edition of this book in 2002, it has become clear that our times are getting even more "uncommon."

> *"In a time of universal deceit, telling the truth is a revolutionary act."*
> *—George Orwell*

Section I, "Weird is the New Normal," introduces you to the weirdness that now seems to be normal in many areas of our lives, and not just the weather. Everywhere we look, things are getting stranger. Global climate change is at the heart of the debate, and what you will learn here may differ significantly from what others want you to believe. Enter this section with an open mind. Arrive at your own conclusions, but common sense suggests that you consider all the evidence first.

> *"Forewarned, forearmed; to be prepared is half the victory."*
> *—Miguel de Cervantes*

Section II, "Preparing for Weirdness," tells you how to intelligently react to any weird events that may visit your life and—first and foremost—how to stay alive. We provide you with easy-to-follow guidance on how to assemble four key resource sets that will increase the likelihood that you and your loved ones will survive the next disaster, whatever it is, and wherever you are. We offer much practical information that reflects new innovations and products that can help you and your loved ones survive disruptions of any kind. By following these proven methods, you can ease your passage through stressful events like severe weather, power outages and disasters—natural and man-made—that are unpredictable and unpreventable, whether we like it or not.

You will also find here reliable information about edible and medicinal wild plants, and herbal, homeopathic and household remedies that you can use for common health symptoms that you may experience when normal support systems are disrupted. "Checklists" (page 143) includes many charts and worksheets to help guide you through your necessary preparations.

> *"The creative individual has the capacity to free himself from the web of social*
> *pressures in which the rest of us are caught.*
> *He is capable of questioning the assumptions that the rest of us accept."*
> *—John W. Gardner*

Section III, "Understanding Weirdness," helps you foresee more clearly into the misty future. It illuminates the big (moving) picture by exploring many examples of why and how fundamental assumptions that we have cherished for centuries are now beginning to fail. By exploring these assumptions about our economy, health, food, water, and other critical life-support areas, we improve our chances of keeping our balance when these areas shift suddenly under our feet, as they surely will.

The more we know and understand, the better prepared we can be to protect the health, safety, and well-being of ourselves and our loved ones in these increasingly uncommon times. We share this information with you because knowledge is power. We want to help you significantly reduce the power of fear in your life by teaching you how to turn potentially deadly situations into something survivable.

Preparation without hope is pointless, and there is much to be hopeful about. Hence, we close Section III with evidence of many positive changes that are occurring ever more rapidly, all over the world. Oftentimes, weirdly enough, it is children who are leading the way.

> *"The wolf also shall dwell with the lamb,*
> *and the leopard shall lie down with the kid;*
> *and the calf and the young lion and the fatling together;*
> *and a little child shall lead them."*
> *—Isaiah 11:6*

Table of Contents

COMMON SENSE;
ADDRESSED TO THE
INHABITANTS
OF
AMERICA;

Section I
Weird is the New Normal

1

Weird is the New Normal

EVERYTHING YOU NEED TO KNOW,
YOU LEARNED FROM NOAH'S ARK...
SOMETIMES THINGS GET REALLY WEIRD.

In late December, 2004, a massive Indian Ocean earthquake released the equivalent energy of 23,000 Hiroshima bombs. The resulting tsunami surprised coastal residents, killing 150,000 and displacing millions more in 11 countries. Brian's daughters lived in Phuket, Thailand, then. The eldest, fortunately, was stateside for a holiday, while the other, following some unspoken inner guidance, moved inland and upstairs just before the event. She survived, but those living where she used to did not. It makes you stop and pause.

In August of 2005, Katrina bore down on New Orleans, breaching ancient levees, stranding people on rooftops, changing the city forever; and people said, "How weird!"

In late 2006, the always-dependable American housing market began to cool. Soon, the sub-prime mortgage market collapsed as home owners walked away from newly unaffordable variable-rate loans, and by mid-2008, after the worst economic collapse since the 1920s, housing prices had declined in almost every US city, and the economy was in free-fall. When the "game" ended, the world narrowly missed another Great Depression. Tax payers bailed out companies deemed "too big to fail," and then lost their jobs and houses in the aftermath; and people said, "Really weird!"

In 2010, Pakistan's Indus River flooded as never before, making 20 million humans homeless; and people said, "Very weird!"

In March of 2011, an enormous earthquake and tsunami caused the Fukushima Daiichi nuclear reactors to do the impossible—melt down—resulting in power shortages and mass evacuations; and people said, "So weird!"

In the summer of 2012, only a year after record flooding along the Mississippi River, Old Man River almost dried up from Cairo to New Orleans. In 2013, it was flooding again; and people said, "That's weird!"

In October of 2012, Sandy, a perfect hybrid storm, larger than Alaska—part hurricane and part blizzard—caused extensive damage as she drove up the east coast. She then went on to devastate coastal areas of New Jersey, New

York and beyond, moving buildings, roads, roller coasters, and boardwalks, filling tunnels and subways, and changing the contours of states. Her waves even shook the earth's crust. Within two weeks Winter Storm Athena pummeled the same area and people said, "Too weird!"

A thoughtful New Jersey victim of too many storms quipped on the evening news, "How many hundred-year storms can we have in six months?" In other words, how often does "weird" have to happen before we all recognize that "Weird is the New Normal"?

In November of 2012, a series of storms, each individually not especially dangerous, lined up as a "Pineapple Express" to lash the normally complacent west coast with storm after storm of cumulatively extraordinary rainfall, snow, and high winds. The winter of 2012-13 featured nearly endless snowstorms for much of the US, followed by a snowy spring; and people said, "How weird!"

In the western US, very low humidity and extraordinary wind velocities sparked wildfires that torched millions of acres and thousands of homes. In early 2013 the National Oceanic and Atmospheric Administration (NOAA) announced that 2012 was the hottest year ever[1] and that people should expect widespread, severe drought[2] in 2013, whose fire season in So. California started very early and fierce, making people say, "Very weird!"

During the winter of 2012-13, people, houses and cars dropped into sink holes. A golfer sank 18' while standing on an Illinois fairway; another man died in Florida after the earth swallowed his bedroom; and a nine-acre sink hole in Louisiana keeps growing, as a salt mine collapses under it, releasing oil and gas into the surrounding air and water; and people said, "Weird."

Before we could recover after the shootings at Sandy Hook Elementary school, two brothers bombed the Boston Marathon on April 15, 2013, That same week, a massive explosion in a fertilizer plant in West, Tex., destroyed most of the town.

In 2013, for the first time ever, snow fell on Arkansas in May. The jet stream, normally placidly pacing around the Arctic, seems lost, diverting hurricanes inland, pouring cold into the south and toasting Minnesota with 97° heat. A 1.5-mile-wide EF5 tornado carved a 17-mile path of destruction through Moore, Okla., on May 20, killing 24, including seven school children, and destroying 4,000 homes and businesses. The debris from the event could cover a basketball court to a depth of 1.7 miles. And seven feet of hail fell in Mexico on May 28, 2013. That seems really weird.

---

1. http://tinyurl.com/2012hottestyear
2. http://tinyurl.com/NOAA2013

What's next? The overdue earthquake that ruptures the San Andreas fault, changing stop-and-go into just plain stop in the fast lanes of Los Angeles and San Francisco? The sudden rush into the sea of enormous ice sheets in Greenland and Antarctica, flooding coastal cities worldwide, making Sandy's inundation of New York just a short preface to a book of many more chapters?

What is going on? For decades forward-looking people have warned of potential disasters ahead for this planet, if we don't change course and pay more respect to the Earth. Such people were dismissed as out-of-touch doom-sayers, but now many see their valid concerns in a clearer light.

Life on Earth is a complex web of interconnections. Every species interacts intimately with others that feed upon it or provide it sustenance. When we cut one small strand, the whole web shudders. That web is our home. Consider an example: In the search for gas, every day we drill 50 new "fracking" wells that contaminate 60% of the nearby water sources and use loud compressors that scare off blue jays that disperse piñon seeds.

Few are concerned about blue jays, but the population of piñon-pine seedlings around fracking wells is now down by 75%, which has reduced the local mouse population, the primary food source for hawks and eagles, whose local populations are lower. With fewer raptors, the rat population is increasing, encouraging the spread of disease, which could decrease the human population, which could, ironically, reduce the need to drill so many "fracking" wells. When we cut the blue jay strand, we endanger ourselves. It's called feedback.

A single strand of a spider web may seem to be superfluous, but Nature is prudent and does not waste resources. Cut enough strands, and the web fails, along with all species that form strands of that web, including humans. And yet we continue to cut strands. We need to *LOL*—Listen, Observe, Learn.

Whether we are dodging a worldwide economic collapse, or the next hundred-year flood, world citizens have been hard hit on many fronts. Today, most people see that Mother Nature has become more extreme. Many wonder whether our actions are hurting the Earth, and, if we damage the only habitable planet we know, whether we will be the ultimate losers.

It may be time to put ourselves at center stage and observe how our actions may be cutting strands in the fragile web of life on Earth—a web that sustains *all of us*. Global cooperation, as if national boundaries and ethnic and religious separations did not exist, will be required if we are to successfully survive long-term as passengers on the same Ark. The difference this time is that this Ark is spinning through space at about 67,000 miles per hour, and both her temperature and water level are rising.

And that is *really* where we are. Now isn't that weird?

2

Global Climate Destabilization

EVERYTHING YOU NEED TO KNOW,
YOU LEARNED FROM NOAH'S ARK...
NO EXPERTS ADVISED HIM.

In 2012, 32,000,000 people were forced to leave their homes due to weather-related reasons.[1] Here is essential information that will help you understand what's happening.

ACIDIFICATION

Carbon dioxide, CO_2, in the atmosphere is increasing, which speeds the formation of carbonic acid in sea water, which makes the oceans more acidic, which kills barrier reefs and the multitudes of beautiful creatures that inhabit them. Here's that feedback again! In the last 30 years, according to Katharina Fabricius, in a report published by the National Academy of Sciences,[2] fully half of Australia's famed Great Barrier Reef has died off. Les Kaufman, one of the scientists involved in the study, said, "The problem is entirely solvable, and coral reefs can be saved through concerted effort over this and the following two or three generations. There is absolutely no excuse for failure to do this, and if we do fail, our generation will forever be remembered for unimaginable, unforgivable stupidity and sloth."

Ocean acidification is the real reason that it is important to control CO_2, because cutting one too many strands in the web of life that supports our species will exterminate us. Global warming from "greenhouse gases," on the other hand, is widely misunderstood, as explained below. Common sense suggests that we reduce all unnatural emissions into our atmosphere, including CO_2, but that we do not make enormous expenditures on drastic measures until we know more clearly what is really going on.

"FRANKENSTORM" SANDY

Whatever the reasons for the undeniably warmer temperatures on Earth,[3] there is a growing unease among its inhabitants that our climate is not as stable and predictable as

1. http://tinyurl.com/32MillionWeatherRefugees
2. http://tinyurl.com/BarrierReefHalfDead
3. http://tinyurl.com/2012hottestyear

it once was. It seems to be coming unglued, and "Frankenstorm" Sandy is a prime example. Several factors may have intensified her impact:

- Warmer oceans contributed to heavier rainfall;

- Higher sea levels created stronger storm surges;

- Arctic melting may be increasing the risk of the kind of "atmospheric traffic jam" that drove Sandy inland; and

- Increased planetary warming may be raising the probability of extreme weather events.

SEVERE-WEATHER EVENTS

When Katrina struck New Orleans in late August, 2005, it carried a storm surge up into the city that breached levees and caused enormous damage and loss of life. Did global warming make it more severe? Like so many processes on Planet Earth, no direct link can be proven, but there is good reason to suspect that it did.

That same year Los Angeles had a 24" snowfall. High winds shut down nuclear power plants in Scandinavia and cut power to hundreds of thousands. The Missouri River hit an all-time low. Europe suffered an intense drought that spawned wild fires. Temperatures in Arizona exceeded 110° for a week, killing 20. Mumbai got 27" of rain in one day, killing 1,000 people. On May 2, 2013, 18" of snow fell in Blooming Prairie, Minn., an all-time record. These events were probably caused or made worse by climate change, and every succeeding year seems to get worse.

VULNERABILITY

Hurricane Sandy demonstrated that extreme-weather events are likely to become more common in a warming world. The dikes, levees, barrier dunes, sea walls, and other structures were built to withstand the relatively mild weather extremes of the last century, but the 21st century is a new ball game.

Extrapolation follows a trend and extends it forward to see where it leads. What is the trend? The climate is getting more extreme on a more frequent basis. On December 6, 2012, the American Geophysical Union[1] reported the conclusions of 140 of our best scientists concerning the Arctic region:

- The 40 largest glaciers lost an area about twice that of the previous decade's annual average.

- Plankton populations have exploded, disrupting the life cycles of many animals from lemmings to Arctic foxes.

---

1. http://tinyurl.com/ArcticReport

- Greenland saw its warmest summer in 170 years.
- The extent of sea ice in the Arctic is the lowest on record.[1]

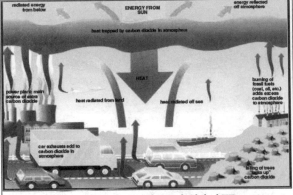

A Too-simple Understanding of Global Warming: CO_2 is like a blanket.

Swedish scientist Svante Arrhenius was the first to claim in 1896 that fossil-fuel combustion may eventually result in enhanced global warming. The topic was relatively inert in the media until ecologist Stephen Schneider in 1976 predicted "global warming" from CO_2 accumulation in the atmosphere. Since then it has been a media circus. The concept of "greenhouse gases" is fairly straightforward (diagram above): visible light from sun passes through the atmosphere to reach the Earth, where some of it becomes heat, some of which is re-emitted in the infrared range of the electromagnetic spectrum.

The problem is that these same "greenhouse" gas molecules, like CO_2 and methane, which allow visible light to pass through without issue, now absorb *some* of the energy when it comes back the other way in the form of heat, *i.e.*, infrared radiation. Visible light can be split by a prism into a rainbow of colors, each of which is a different frequency. Infrared light can also be split into frequencies, but we cannot see any of its "colors."

The frequencies of infrared that block heat are determined by the orbital structures of the molecules of the "greenhouse" gas. An electron in orbit around the nucleus of a molecule can pop into a higher orbit if it can absorb a precise amount of energy called a quantum. When a molecule is struck by a photon of the right frequency, it absorbs a quantum of energy and bounces the electron up to the next orbit, exciting and warming the molecule, which then warms the atmosphere a tiny bit. If the photon is some other frequency, it passes through the molecule and does not warm it. Most of the frequencies of infrared radiation cannot be absorbed, and they pass through to outer space, just as visible light would.

---

1. http://tinyurl.com/SeaIceMax2013

Methane

It is often said[1] that methane (CH_4) is 100 times more effective than CO_2 as a "greenhouse gas," and enormous concentrations of organic material in the permafrost regions are expected to decompose as the climate warms, releasing methane into the atmosphere, swamping the CO_2 effect. If "greenhouse gases" are a problem, then methane, rather than CO_2, is the culprit to watch. So let's look at methane in more depth.

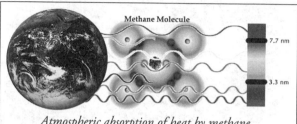

Because of its molecular structure, methane absorbs only in two regions, 3.3 nm and 7.7 nm, as seen here.[2] If infrared (heat) radiation trying to leave the Earth encounters a methane molecule, the wave-

Atmospheric absorption of heat by methane. Black absorption bands are the shadows of methane.

lengths that can energize methane electrons are absorbed, leaving black shadows in the infrared spectrum called absorption lines.

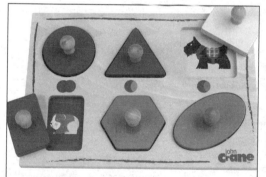

Like a toy in which only a specific shape fits into a given hole, only specific frequencies of infrared radiation can be absorbed by a greenhouse-gas molecule.

The critical question related to the global-warming debate concerns what happens when the concentration of a greenhouse gas is increased. The too-simple understanding that you might draw from the diagram on page 6 suggests that "greenhouse gases" are like a blanket on the Earth, keeping her warm. We all know that when we pull up a second blanket at night, we feel warmer, so if we double the concentration of "greenhouse gases," the Earth should warm in a corresponding manner, which would seem to be a reason to reduce greenhouse gas concentrations in the atmosphere. But that is too simple.

It may help to think of greenhouse-gas absorption of infrared energy like a baby's shape toy. Only square shapes fit into square holes in the frame. (Only

---

1. http://tinyurl.com/MethaneArctic
2. A nanometer, or nm, is also a micron, a very tiny measure of distance.

certain frequencies can get absorbed.) Think of the frame as warming up 1°
every time a correct shape is placed into the right hole. Basketballs and marbles
do not warm the frame. (Wrong frequencies escape into outer space).

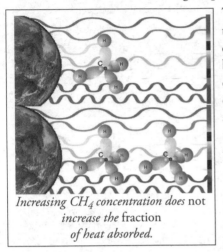

*Increasing CH_4 concentration does not
increase the fraction
of heat absorbed.*

The first key insight is this: Almost all of
the available shapes (infrared frequencies) are like basketballs and marbles—they do not fit the holes. They
escape the Earth, are not trapped, and
do not warm the atmosphere. The
absorption bands are a small fraction of
the total infrared spectrum.

The second key insight is this: doubling
the frames a baby can choose from may
shorten the time she needs to find a hole
that fits the shape she holds, but it does
not allow a given shape to get stuck in
more than one frame, nor does it allow
triangles to suddenly fit into square holes. The same frequencies get absorbed
in the same way, regardless of the concentration of the methane in the atmosphere.

Doubling the concentration of "greenhouse gases" is like doubling the
frames a baby can put a shape into. It will cut the time a quantum takes to find
a molecule to accept it, but it will not increase what frequencies (shapes) will
get absorbed. The same *fraction* of the infrared spectrum gets absorbed in
either case; the absorption shadows are identical; and it is *only* by increasing the
fraction of energy absorbed (enlarging the shadows) that the Earth's atmosphere
can be warmed by increasing "greenhouse gas concentrations.

At any concentration, a given photon of heat energy is absorbed in the
atmosphere, warming it by the same amount. It gets absorbed because its frequency is exactly right to lift an electron of the greenhouse molecule to a
higher orbit. This is quantum physics, which may be why it is hard to understand, but now you do!

SUPPORTING DATA

Esteemed scientific journal *Nature* in 1971 published data from Antarctic
ice cores that date back 450,000 years, concluding, "Changes in CO_2 content
in the atmosphere *never* precede changes in air temperature." Never.

So, as long as we still live in a cause-and-effect universe, the implication is
that the current well-documented rise in global temperatures cannot be

explained by recent rises in CO_2 in the atmosphere. But please remember that increasing CO_2 (see above) does acidify the oceans, which all by itself can eliminate human life on Earth, so we must conclude that it is still important to reduce atmospheric CO_2 if we wish to survive long term. Solar energy still trumps fossil-fuel energy in this respect.

SOLAR WARMING

So, if "greenhouse gases" are not warming the Earth, then what *is*? There have been some interesting and potentially relevant alternate theories and information related to temperature rises on our sister solar satellites, which might point the finger to our sun as the primary culprit. The data is sparse and not yet definitive—not every heavenly body in our solar system is well measured in this respect—but these are some points to consider:

- Mars: Surface temperatures are rising, quickly melting the ice caps. Russian astronomer Habibullo Abdussamatov says the simultaneous warming of Earth and Mars is no coincidence, and that the increased intensity of solar radiation explains both.[1]

- Imke de Pater and Philip Marcus of UC Berkeley in a 2006 joint study of Jupiter[2] concluded that images of a new spot suggests the planet is in the midst of a global change that could increase temperatures by as much as 10°F on different parts of its surface.

- In a multi-author 1998 study sponsored by NASA, NSF, and the National Geographic, researchers reported that the Hubble Space Telescope has found that Neptune's largest moon, Triton, has heated up significantly since Voyager visited it in 1989.[3]

- Tiny Pluto seems to be rising in temperature in its thin and cold atmosphere, even though it is moving farther from the Sun on its long, odd-shaped orbit.[4]

- Researchers Henrik Svensmark[5] and Nigel Calder place the sun, stars, and cosmic rays at center stage in the climate-change debate.

- Danish astronomer Eigil Friis-Christensen concludes that increases in solar activity reduce cloud formation, allowing more cosmic rays to penetrate, thus warming the Earth.[6]

1. http://tinyurl.com/MarsWarming
2. http://tinyurl.com/JupiterWarming
3. http://tinyurl.com/TritonWarming
4. http://tinyurl.com/PlutoWarming
5. Svensmark, in bibliography, page 158.

The scientific work reviewed here will not settle the issue of "greenhouse gases," but it may help open for discussion the topic of whether or not the sun is the major player in this drama. If it is, as it appears to us, then common sense suggests that the enormous funding that is poised to be spent on mitigating "greenhouse gases" might be more wisely spent building dikes or moving people back from the coasts, where sea levels are already on the rise.

CHEM TRAILS

There is a related topic that does not seem to fade—chem trails. In recent years more and more people have been reporting unidentified jets spewing something into the high atmosphere in patterns that do not dissipate quickly.[1] Many see a conspiracy, but there is a perspective to consider, relevant to our discussions of global warming.

We do not claim to know more than anyone else, but if *we* can read about how the sun is warming the planets, then so can others, like government agencies and the military. If they conclude that global warming comes from too much solar-energy influx, they might experiment with trying to reduce it by creating bright, persistent con trails high in the sky—artificial clouds. "Chem trails" may be just that, and some day we may need such artificial clouds to protect all of us from some serious solar baking. It may be a far-fetched theory, but, like the chem trails themselves, the perspective persists.

If increasing the concentration of greenhouse gases in the atmosphere cannot change the *fraction* of infrared energy absorbed, and yet the planet is still warming, then either the incoming energy is increasing, which seems likely, or we are increasing the amount of heat we are putting into the atmosphere, or we are increasing the fraction of the incoming solar energy that we are converting to heat. Or all of the above, which is most likely.

What can we do?

- We can reduce our overall energy consumption, which dumps heat into the air. Reducing energy demand reduces the dumping of heat by nuclear and other power plants.

- We can drive less, as our engines produce heat.

- We can leave stubble on agricultural fields rather than plowing them in the fall, which is done to warm the earth sooner in the spring, so that planting can start earlier, so as to produce larger yields.

---

6. http://tinyurl.com/SolarWarming
1. http://tinyurl.com/videoChem-Trail

- We can use more reflective concrete and less asphalt on roads.
- We can do less paving and more greening.
- We can set our air conditioners warmer in the summer, especially restaurants and other public establishments that are so cold that customers need to wear jackets "inside" in the summer.
- We can heat our homes less in the winter.
- We can plant trees.

According to NASA,[1] dark rooftops can be 42° F hotter than white ones. We can paint black roofs white, which can reduce air-conditioning demand as much as 20%. Concordia University estimated that painting 1% of the world's urban surfaces white (rooftops and pavement) could reduce CO_2 emissions by 130 gigatons over the next century.

Juan Carlos, founder of the White Roof Project,[2] a New York City non-profit that harnesses volunteers to provide roof-painting services, says painting 5% of the world's rooftops white per year by 2030 could save enough emissions to equal the world's current annual carbon output.

- We can work with local building codes to promote white roofs.

GAIA

There is a school of thought that regards the Earth as a living being—her bones are mountain ranges, and her bodily fluids are oil, water, and air. J.E. Lovelock[3] coined the term in 1967, and it is instructive to look at climate destabilization from a Gaian perspective. When Gaia gets too warm from too much sun, she perspires by evaporating water, which cools the oceans and creates white clouds that reduce sunlight. When she is ill, she runs a temperature, which we call global warming. When her liquids and solids are drained, does it cause her surface to subsides creating sink holes? It may be a stretch for some to consider a living being as massive as our planet, but it should be clear that *if* the Earth is alive, then common sense would encourage us not to insult her so much that she begins shaking us off like so many fleas.

---

1. http://tinyurl.com/PaintRoofsWhite
2. http://tinyurl.com/WhiteRoofProject video
3. Lovelock, page 158.

Section II
Preparing for Weirdness

3

Staying Alive

EVERYTHING YOU NEED TO KNOW,
YOU LEARNED FROM NOAH'S ARK...
IF YOU'RE NOT ON BOARD, THE REST DOESN'T MATTER.

The Bee Gees had it right. It's all about "stayin' alive." If you fail on that task, anything else we have to offer in this book will be moot. The airlines have it right, too:

Adults first.

TIP
PUT ON YOUR OWN MASK FIRST.

You must take care of yourself before you can be of service to others. You cannot help others in a crisis if you are dead or incapacitated.

TIP
IF YOU PLAN TO BE IN A MASS PUBLIC EVENT LIKE THE BOSTON MARATHON,
AVOID METAL CONTAINERS LIKE MAILBOXES AND DUMPSTERS.
STAY IN THE OPEN.

We live in a changing world where the rate of change seems to accelerate daily. Sometimes it is hard to remember yesterday's disaster, since so many new ones appear so quickly. And the weather seems to be getting more extreme. One day is balmy and the next is snowy. "Weird is the New Normal."

This nation changed greatly after 9/11/2001, beefing up security at airports and raising the level of our collective awareness and preparedness. Still, disasters continue to happen, some natural, some intentional, and unfortunately, we don't see an end to it soon. If you are bleeding from a gunshot or a homemade bomb exploding, you probably do not care much about the political persuasion of the perpetrator.

If you are a relative of one of the 500 or so annual victims of street homicides in Chicago, you probably will find little consolation in someone's placing political blame for the event on some designated bad person or group.

If you are terrified by someone's actions, that person, by definition, is a terrorist.

TIP
BE ESPECIALLY ALERT ON CALENDAR DATES THAT MIGHT BE ATTRACTIVE
TARGETS FOR TERRORISTS: 9/11, PATRIOT'S DAY, JULY 4TH, *ETC.* [1]

In short, you might find your life disturbed at any time in any number of ways, and these disruptions can come largely without warning, with well-forecast hurricanes being the exception. This book will give you a logical and organized way to deal with the kinds of unplanned changes that might invade your tranquility at any moment.

The man who is prepared has his battle half fought.
—Miguel De Cervantes

What Can We Do?

After the Boston Marathon bombings of April 15, 2013, Tom Ridge, former Director of Homeland Security, advised people as follows:

TIP
IF YOU SEE SOMETHING, SAY SOMETHING!

We agree. Stay alert and do your part. We are our brothers' keepers. And our sisters', too. It's how we humans survive.

Imagine that you are standing on a railroad crossing, enjoying the view, and the thunder in the earth feels like a good foot massage. Your common sense screams at you to forego the view and the foot massage and just get off the tracks, for danger is here. Your ego warns that others might think you gullible or fearful if you flee some unproven danger, and your intellect demands that you make no move before reading the long-awaited, definitive results of the Independent National Railway Safety Committee's study[2] on whether vibrations in the earth caused by fast trains constitute any real danger to public health and safety or endangered species. It is a free country, and it is your choice whether or not heed your common sense. It's priceless.

TIP
COMMON SENSE PRECEDES SCIENTIFIC STUDIES.
TO STAY ALIVE, HEED YOUR COMMON SENSE.
IT IS FREE AND IMMEDIATE, AND IT DOES NOT MISLEAD.

---

1. The Boston Marathon bombers had planned on July 4.
2. an imaginary research study secretly funded by the railroad industry.

4

Four Key Resource Sets

EVERYTHING YOU NEED TO KNOW, YOU LEARNED FROM NOAH'S ARK...
SPEED IS NOT ALWAYS AN ADVANTAGE—
THE SNAILS WERE ON BOARD WITH THE CHEETAHS.

The four types of short-term emergencies and their corresponding resource sets depend upon where you are when times become very "uncommon":

- **Away from home**

Without a vehicle: Pocket Set

In your vehicle: Pocket Set, Vehicle Box, and Go Pack

- **At home**

Stuck at home, no utilities: Pocket Set, Stash, Vehicle Box, and Go Pack

Evacuated from home: Pocket Set, Portable Stash, Vehicle Box, and Go Pack

AWAY FROM HOME, WITHOUT A VEHICLE

You're walking or traveling by public transportation, and suddenly crisis erupts. Perhaps it is an earthquake, a car accident, a tornado, or a fire. You have nothing but what is on your person. *Do the common-sense thing every day*:

TIP
KEEP WITH YOUR KEYS A FEW SMALL ESSENTIALS THAT WILL HELP
YOU SURVIVE AN UNEXPECTED EMERGENCY.

Pocket Set

The *Pocket Set* includes, in descending order of importance for most folks: your key set, a charged-up cell phone, some water, a whistle, a large bandana or handkerchief, and a small pocket knife or multi-purpose tool. Survival bracelets comprised of braided paracord with a whistle in the latch are available online for about $5.00. A little cord is always useful and a whistle can call for help.

A bottle of **water,** used sparingly, can extend your life by up to 12 days under certain conditions. We recommend that you routinely carry good water with you, which most people do because of the increased uncertainty of the safety, taste and even availability of public drinking-water supplies.

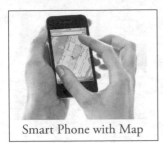

Smart Phone with Map

Cell phones—what would we do without them? We are all well aware of how important it can be to be trackable, especially if we are caught in a snow drift or under rubble after an earthquake. Authorities can track your cell phone. Perhaps you are someone who prefers not to be trackable. That is your choice, but it carries inherent risks.

An individual staying in the Hotel Montana during the massive 7.0 richter-scale earthquake in Port-au-Prince, Haiti, in January, 2010, was caught under rubble and seriously injured, but he saved his own life by using an app on his smart phone. Trapped in darkness and knowing he needed to find a safer place with a little more structure to help brace for aftershocks, he began taking pictures with his smart-phone camera, whose flash exposed the otherwise-pitch-black surroundings. Once he found a safe place to await rescue, he found his leg broken and blood running from his head. Luckily, a smart-phone app he had downloaded earlier advised him on how to treat wounds, which he did without injuring himself further. Then, almost two days later, rescue workers pulled him from the debris.[1] Cell phones save lives, so try to keep yours fully charged before leaving home.

A **whistle** can call for help or deter an attacker. A **bandana** or handkerchief, in addition to many daily uses, makes an impromptu face mask that filters out some of the dust and noxious fumes, especially if it is wet. If you are desperate and without water, you can urinate on the cloth. Although distasteful, fresh urine is sterile and can be used to stay alive. Be clear about priorities.

TIP

IT IS BETTER TO LIVE BY DRINKING URINE THAN TO DIE OF THIRST.

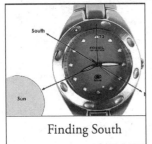

Finding South

A small **pocket knife** or a multi-use tool set with some blades, a small pliers, a pair of scissors, some screw drivers, *etc.*, can be very useful in countless ways, and it may save your life. We recommend that you carry a pocket knife that is allowed on board an aircraft, which is non-locking and no more than 2.36" long. This rule could change, so get current with rules before flying.

Most smart phones can show you directions, but cell phones fail or lose signal. If you wish, carry a small, inexpensive **compass**, but there are other ways. In the Northern Hemisphere, hold or imagine holding an

---

1. http://thedailyupbeat.com

analog watch flat on the earth, with the hour hand pointing in the direction of the sun. Bisect (cut in half) the angle between the hour hand and the 12:00 (1:00 during daylight savings time) mark to get the north-south line. Find south along that line toward the sun. A similar but reversed method works in the Southern Hemisphere.

TIP

DON'T PANIC. KEEPING CALM ALLOWS YOUR COMMON SENSE AND
INTUITION TO SURFACE AND LEAD YOU TO A SAFE PLACE.

Even easier, if the sky is clear at night, look for Polaris in the sky to find north. Find it by following the two stars in the front lip of the big Dipper. They point up to the North Star, which has guided people for centuries.

AWAY FROM HOME, IN YOUR VEHICLE

You are on the road, late at night, and your engine dies, or you run off the road and disable your vehicle, miles from nowhere. Your cell phone shows no signal. What should you have in your vehicle?

The answer to that question obviously depends upon your local climate and other requirements that only you can determine. If you're on the side of the road in International Falls in January, for example, warmth will be a higher concern than food.

In your vehicle you should plan on having two separate sets of emergency items: your *Go Pack* and your *Vehicle Box*. The *Go Pack* goes with you if you have to leave the vehicle in an emergency, and it contains items that can sustain you without other supplies for 72 hours or so. The *Vehicle Box* stays with the vehicle at all times and contains items useful in maintaining the vehicle. Do not assume that public transportation will be available, on time, or safe during an emergency. Know alternate road routes, because your favorite route may be blocked.

Go Pack list: see page 145.

Vehicle Box list: see page 147

TIP

EXPLORE ALTERNATE ROUTES WHENEVER YOU HAVE TIME.

Go Pack

The **Go Pack** starts with a comfortable back pack, such as a student book bag, large enough to carry your chosen essentials without being so heavy as to sabotage your ability to hike out of danger with it when the time comes. So choose wisely, selecting small, light items if you have any choice. To reduce costs, it is recommended that you stock your *Go Pack* with extra or old clothing items, and free or inexpensive supplies, whenever possible. For example, buy a student back pack on clearance sale, or find one at a thrift store. You may even have extras lying around. It's function, not fashion, that you seek.

If a working smart phone with maps is not an option, you can still be OK if you think ahead. Buy a map or get on any computer that has Internet access and surf to Google Maps.[1] Find your home and other neighborhoods you are often in, and print out detailed maps of those areas. (Remember that ink-jet printouts are water soluble. Use a laser if you can.) Be sure to display both roads and terrain, as roads are usually faster, but you may have to cross the countryside on foot, in which case you need to know how to avoid the hazards. We recommend that you keep these maps folded up in your *Go Pack* in a plastic zip-lock baggy. Wet maps are useless.

Refer to the check list of recommended items for the *Go Pack* (page 145), which is in descending order of priority for most people in most places. You are encouraged to add and delete items and change their priorities, according to your perceived needs. Keep your *Go Pack* complete. If you need to rob it, restore it as soon as you can. Your life may depend upon it, as the following story illustrates.

Reshma Begum was miraculously saved from the rubble of the April 24, 2013, Bangladesh clothing-factory collapse 17 days after the accident.[2] She had been banging on pipes to make noise and calling out to rescue workers, before she was finally heard. At the time of her rescue, a demolition crew was beginning to raze the building.

As the building began to collapse, she had rushed down a stairwell into the basement, where she had become trapped in a triangle of safety, which provided her space to survive. Initially, her long hair was stuck in rubble, but she found a sharp object to cut it and freed herself. Luckily, she had dried food, which she ate for 15 days, and some bottles of water, which she rationed, which kept her alive. With a pocket knife in your *Pocket Set* and water and dried food in your *Go Pack*, you, too, should have enough to survive a situation like this.

Vehicle Box

The **Vehicle Box** is typically a plastic storage bin that you keep stowed somewhere in your vehicle, equipped in a useful way. It is assumed that your vehicle already has a normal emergency set of spare tire, jack, and tire iron.

---

1. https://maps.google.com
2. http://tinyurl.com/ABCNews17DaySurvival

Refer to the prioritized list of recommended items for your *Vehicle Box* (See page 147) in which you will find suggested quantities.

Fuel

We have some people in our family who like to keep their gas tank almost full so they never have to worry about running out of gas. They have reason for this, since they have experienced running out of gas at the most inopportune moment. (But when was it ever good to run out of gas?)

Because the price of gas has been high, many people put off filling the tank. However, it is cheaper to keep it full, due to reduced surface evaporation in the tank, and it is also good to keep your tank close to full in case you have to make a break for it at some unpredictable point. During a crisis, you can count on long lines at gas stations, if any are open at all. Katrina closed refineries, causing *severe* gas shortages throughout the southeast. During Frankenstorm Sandy, gasoline supplies ran out throughout the region. Just because a disaster is not in your area does not mean you cannot be affected by it.

TIP

IF A STRANGER APPROACHES YOUR CAR,
LOCK YOUR DOORS AND LOWER THE WINDOW ENOUGH TO TALK,
BUT NOT SO FAR AS TO ALLOW HIM TO REACH IN TO OPEN THE DOOR.

Stash

With every passing year, our more chaotic weather brings more storms, tornados, fires, droughts and floods. In the middle of your daily routine at home, perhaps your lights go out, followed by no water pressure. Your battery-powered radio tells you to stay indoors. What should you have on hand?

We suggest that you start now to accumulate a *Stash* of emergency materials and store it in your home. As you build your *Stash*, divide it into two portions—the part that goes with you when you evacuate, and the rest of it, which will typically be useful things too heavy or bulky to carry, such as collections of canned goods and extra containers of water. If you are a city dweller without a vehicle, you will rely more on your *Go Pack* and you will prepare your *Stash* for use in your home.

Your stay-at-home *Stash* might be well located in your *Safehaven Room*, a carefully selected and prepared room in which you may have to seal yourself and your loved ones during a toxic-air episode. If you don't have a room you can set up, designate a closet where you can take your portable *Stash* with water, food and a few essentials for the short term.

> Safehaven Room:
> See page 37.

19

The portable *Stash* is best stored in a car-top carrier or inexpensive plastic storage bins, depending on your needs, storage space and vehicle capacity. It is akin to preparing for an instant camping trip. Store it where it will be easy to load into your vehicle, in containers that are liftable by folks who might need to do so. If you get stuck at home, the entire *Stash* will be available to you. Don't wait for an emergency before building and sorting out your two stashes.

Refer to the prioritized list of important items to be stored in your *Stash* (page 148). Password *hints* for important online account access can be recorded on page 157. Another critical item is *copies* of important papers, including family records, birth and marriage certificates, wills, contracts, deeds, bank account numbers and financial records, stocks, bonds, insurance policies, passports, social-security cards, immunization records, credit-card account numbers, and inventory of valuables. But before you make a pile of copies, consider the following.

Identity Theft

Each year 15 million US citizens have their identities stolen, with an average financial loss of about $3,500. If you keep the location of your *Stash* locked, you need to make sure that you can get access to it quickly when you need to, but if the location is not secure, an intruder could steal your identity from your *Stash*, so it might be wiser to keep the copies in a safety-deposit box and keep the key where you can retrieve it easily. A home-grown alternative is to plastic-wrap them and store them in your refrigerator or freezer, or some other safe location. A high-tech choice is to use an online-storage service. We use DropBox.com, which is one of many.[1]

TIP

KEEP IN YOUR *STASH* COPIES OF YOUR FAVORITE PICTURES,
READY TO TAKE WITH YOU.

If you are computer-savvy, store your best pictures and videos online at some free site like justcloud,[2] photobucket,[3] shutterfly,[4] or icloud,[5] although access to a computer or smartphone to access them is unlikely in worst-case scenarios.

---

1. http://tinyurl.com/5CloudStorageOptions
2. http://www.justcloud.com
3. http://photobucket.com
4. http://www.shutterfly.com
5. http://tinyurl.com/Apple-iCloud-Storage

EVACUATED FROM HOME

In the 1970s Pam lived in Cyprus with her Marine husband and their young son. Periodic skirmishes between the Greeks and Turks on the island were not uncommon. One night the Cypriot President's helicopter was shot down. Expecting trouble, military authorities knocked on all the doors of military personnel and informed them to pack one suitcase and be ready to go in 30 minutes... "*and you may not be returning!*"

Pam threw some of her son's things in the suitcase, plus a few clothes, some good pieces of jewelry, and a photo album. What would *you* take right now if you had to leave in 30 minutes? This was an unusual circumstance, but people in the 2012 Colorado fires had less time than that to evacuate.

Perhaps a nuclear power plant has melted down upwind from you, and deadly radioactive fallout is coming your way, or a chemical plant has exploded nearby. You may have to leave your home for an extended period, and there is too little time to start packing. Your *Stash* will supply you with needed items whether you are at a shelter or someone else's home.

A visiting couple told us of a friend whose rural California neighborhood was burned out by a wild fire. The friend was able to pack and leave quickly (wheels on fire!), but a neighbor chose to use valuable time to gather pictures, pets, and documents. The neighbor never made it out, nor did seven others, but if they had had their portable stashes ready to load into their fueled and properly pointed vehicles, they might still be with us.

TIP

THE RIGHT TIME TO BEGIN TO PREPARE IS NOT
WHEN AN EMERGENCY IS IN YOUR FACE—THE TIME IS NOW.

BEING PREPARED

If you are following the advice of this book, you will have your *Pocket Set* with you, and your *Go Pack* will be in your vehicle. You quickly load your *Portable Stash* into your vehicle. Turn off the natural gas, water and power in the house, which you have previously located, and get out of town without delay, driving carefully and confidently, using well-known alternate routes where necessary. Your vehicle should be fueled and in good condition, with its *Vehicle Box* in order.

Stash items
See page 148.

Do I need to evacuate?
See page 34.

Plan your escape routes carefully, beforehand. Airborne danger is most likely to come from upwind, which is often a southwesterly direction. Plan to first travel away from danger, in a cross-wind direction. Obvious routes clog quickly, which is why we suggest knowing your back roads. Memorize landmarks because street lights and signs may not be functioning. You may want to mark the planned routes on road maps in your *Vehicle Box* or *Go Pack*.

Coordinate with family members on these important topics:

- how to get out of your home in an emergency;
- where to meet nearby outside your home;
- where to meet outside your neighborhood; and
- several places to meet out of town, one in each major direction.
- designate one place as the default place, in case there is no reason to go in any particular direction.

Where to meet
See page 153.

Cell phone list
See page 143

It is best to work this process out before an emergency. We have included forms (side box) on which you may record places to meet and everyone's current cell phone numbers, so you can coordinate with each other.

PETS AND ANIMALS

Pets and their needs raise a sensitive question that many of us will not want to honestly address—if evacuating your pets would endanger your life and your family's, would you do it anyway? This is a most difficult decision for anyone who loves their pets—and we have several beloved, irreplaceable, four-leggeds in our house. Depending on your situation, deciding to evacuate your pets may make your mission much more difficult or even impossible. Quite often with expected disasters such as hurricanes, pet shelters will be set up, so check with the local authorities.

Clarify your priorities in advance and plan accordingly. We recommend that you prepare a separate *Pet Stash* that can be easily loaded and taken with you, if, at the time, you decide to do that.

TIP
YOUR LIFE IS THE HIGHEST PRIORITY, AND YOUR PET MAY BE ABLE
TO FEND FOR ITSELF FOR A WHILE.

If you have to leave your pet, and it cannot be left outside, inform someone you know outside the disaster area that your pets are inside your home. Do this *en route*, not before you leave. Every second may count.

5

Earth

EVERYTHING YOU NEED TO KNOW, YOU LEARNED FROM NOAH'S ARK...
WE ALL SEEK SOLID GROUND.

DRIVING CAN BE HAZARDOUS

One of the most treacherous activities we engage in is driving across the surface of our Earth. Each year nearly 40,000 people die on US highways, but fortunately the annual death rate has been falling recently, due to seat belts, better safety standards, designated drivers, and safer vehicles.

TIP
IF YOU CANNOT AVOID A COLLISION, DO NOT SWERVE.
APPLY YOUR BRAKES EVENLY, BRACE AND HEAD RIGHT INTO IT.
VEHICLES CAN ABSORB IMPACT FROM THE FRONT, NOT THE SIDE.

The human brain really doesn't multi-task well. It rotates its attention among all competing items. You travel 88' every second at 60 mph. Giving one second of attention to your phone can kill someone. Some states require the use of headphones to use cell phones while driving. Without them, just talking on a cell phone removes half of your strength from the steering wheel, which you may need if you hit something, someone hits you or you have a blowout.

TIP
DO NOT CALL ON YOUR CELL PHONE OR TEXT WHILE DRIVING.

Recent research shows that hands-free cell phones distract drivers more than a passenger does. A group of 41 people, mostly young adults, were paired with 41 conversation partners in a driving simulator. They navigated a 24-mile stretch of Interstate under three different driving conditions—alone in the car, talking with a passenger, and talking to someone via a hands-free cell phone. They were told to exit at a specified rest area eight miles into the trip, but those talking on the cell phone were four times more likely to miss the exit and more likely to make other errors like drifting out of their lanes.

TIP
AVOID DRIVING AFTER MIDNIGHT OR WHEN YOU ARE TIRED.

According to a New Zealand study, drivers who slept less than five hours the previous night increased their chances of an accident by 170%.[1] Drinking some coffee or an energy drink, or taking a short walk can help, but studies show that keeping the window open or the radio cranked up does not really keep you reliably awake.

TIP
**WHILE DRIVING BESIDE PARKED VEHICLES,
SURVEY EACH ONE FOR A CHILD RUNNING OUT OR
ANYONE WHO MIGHT SUDDENLY OPEN A DOOR.**

When we are driving, we unconsciously survey our environment for threats, and it does not frighten us to do so. We can carry that attitude into the rest of our lives, always being alert, looking for exits, silently building escape plans. It is not paranoia. It is just common sense.

EARTHQUAKES

While earthquakes can happen anywhere at anytime, you know when you are living in an earthquake-prone area, and you have probably prepared yourself for such eventualities. But earthquakes can occur anywhere. On April 16, 2013, a magnitude-4.3 earthquake shook normally quake-free Oklahoma in the middle of the night.

Most injuries and deaths in earthquakes are caused by loose objects falling out of cabinets, bookcases or other storage areas. Additionally, plants, wall clocks, artwork and pictures can be tossed around.

TIP
**WALK THROUGH YOUR LIVING SPACE AND SECURE ANYTHING THAT MIGHT
HURT SOMEONE IF IT FLEW AROUND DURING AN EARTHQUAKE.**

It can be useful to secure shelves and large cabinets to walls. Attaching lips to shelves can keep small items from sliding off. Brace heavy light fixtures to ceiling joists and install latches on cabinet doors. Secure water heaters, furnaces, gas appliances, and refrigerators to wall studs, because they can cause severe injuries if they fall. Do not expect door frames or windows to operate properly, as they may get warped. Glass can shatter, showering broken glass about, so stay clear of glass during an earthquake. Roof joists can be secured with hurricane clips, which is good safety for stormy areas as well.

Do not expect the electricity to work, so always keep a working flashlight handy. Do not be surprised if the sprinkler system or fire alarm turns on. Do not expect your cell phone or land line to work.

---

1. http://www.rodale.com/distracted-drivers

TIP
**KEEP YOUR HALLWAYS AND EXITS CLEAR OF OBJECTS THAT
MIGHT MAKE IT DIFFICULT TO GET OUT OF THE BUILDING.**

At the first inkling of an earthquake, quickly and safely get outside, if you can. If you can't get out, stay away from anything that can topple, or stand under a doorway. If you have to leave the scene and can reach your vehicle (keys in your *Pocket Set*), you should find there your *Go Pack* (page 145), which can sustain you for a while. Keep this book in your *Go Pack*, and keep your list of rendezvous sites up to date (page 153). With all that, you are ready to go. Make your way as best you can to the default rendezvous site that seems most appropriate, unless circumstances suggest another.

TIP
**ALWAYS PUT YOUR KEYS IN THE SAME PLACE
SO YOU CAN FIND THEM IN A HURRY.**

With buildings collapsing around you, one simple understanding is worth knowing. Buildings are, in most cases, built from beams and slabs, which means that when they collapse, these long pieces tend to form triangular pockets beneath them, in which you can sometimes find safety. This zone is called *the triangle of safety*, and it is taught as standard knowledge in Japan and other earthquake-prone regions around the world.

A young man saved by the triangle of safety.
Credit: AP

When your surroundings are crumbling, and you cannot get outside, find anything strong and lie *beside* it, face down, and cover your head with your arms. A sofa will do, or a solid bathtub. A refrigerator can be good, if it does not topple on you. A chest freezer is excellent.

Do not get *under* anything. Sheltering near a kitchen may provide a life-saving water leak, or some food. FEMA has assembled much useful information about earthquake preparedness that you should read, if you are in an earthquake-prone area.[1]

---

1. http://tinyurl.com/FEMAearthquakes

HURRICANES AND TORNADOES

We will not go into much detail with hurricanes and tornadoes, because those of you who live in such areas know how to prepare for them. If you are visiting an area where a hurricane is coming, you will have time to evacuate, or you will be in a hotel that will advise you of what to do. If you are visiting a tornado area, here are some signs to watch for and things to do if you spot one:

Find shelter if you see any of the following:

- A dark or greenish sky
- Large hail
- A large, dark, low-lying cloud, especially if it's rotating
- A loud roar that sounds like a freight train.

If you are in your automobile do the following:

- Drive to the closest sturdy shelter.
- If your auto is hit by flying debris, pull over and park.
- Stay in the car with your seat belt on. Put your head down below the windows while covering your head with your hands, a blanket, coat or anything you have in the car that can provide protection.
- If you can safely get to a place that is noticeably lower than the level of the roadway, leave your car and lie in that area, covering your head with your hands or any cushioning.

TIP
ALWAYS LOOK FOR A TRIANGLE OF SAFETY.

- Do not get under an overpass or bridge— a low, flat location is safer.
- Never try to use a vehicle to outrun a tornado in urban or congested areas. Instead, leave the vehicle immediately for a safe shelter.
- Watch out for flying debris, which causes most casualties.[1]

TIP
KEEP A CUSHION IN YOUR CAR IN CASE YOU NEED TO SLEEP THERE.

GPS

Growing numbers of people are being led astray by GPS devices whose databases for remote areas like Death Valley have maps that haven't been updated in years. Even in populated areas, such as our rural county in North Carolina, house guests who depend

---

1. http://www.ready.gov/tornadoes

on an older GPS to find us drive miles past us, because the county renumbered all houses a few years back, but the commercial databases did not pick up on it for years. If you use a GPS, we recommend that you update its database annually. Garmin GPS databases, *e.g.,* can be updated online[1] for $50, or $90 for a lifetime of quarterly updates. There is an empty list on page 156 that you may want to copy and make into a To-Do list for tasks like GPS updates.

CHARGING CELL PHONES

Tragically, cell-phone reception is often lost in remote areas, depriving you of a device you may depend on to keep yourself from getting lost. Once lost, you have only what is in your head, on your person, and in your vehicle, which, if you follow our recommendations, should enable you to survive long enough to get back to civilization.

A Micro-USB port standard

If you use a cell phone, another simple path to ruin is to set out on a road trip without a vehicle-based cell-phone charger. Make sure that each cell phone in your group has a charger. Currently, there are about 30 incompatible styles, but help is on the way. The Micro-USB port is the dominant charger style that is usable across many smart phones. The European Union has already made this port its standard, and the US has lined up behind the idea as well,

BioLite CampStove
USB charger

although Apple has introduced a non-standard Lightning connector with its iPhone 5 that prevents third-party cables from being used to charge it.

Solar-powered cell-phone battery chargers are available online.[2] One model costs less than $10.50 and charges most portable devices via a full set of interface plugs. Keep one in your *Go Pack*. BioLite[3] offers a wood-powered generator with a Micro-USB port for recharging off the grid during an overcast period, but it is not very portable.

---

1. http://tinyurl.com/GarminUpdates
2. http://tinyurl.com/SolarCellChargers
3. http://tinyurl.com/WoodUSBcharger

6

Air

Pam is not what you might call disaster-prone, really. However, at 4:00 a.m., April 18, 1979, she and her family were sleeping peacefully at home in Reading, Penn., 50 miles downwind from an as-yet-unfamiliar nuclear power plant called Three Mile Island.

Without so much as a terrorist to blame it on, an unplanned steam release shrieked, awakening the neighbors around the plant. Deadly radioactivity began to boil into the dark skies, moving stealthily and invisibly into the surrounding areas. A plume of deadly air began to move downwind towards Pam and her family. As it happened, they were about to leave on vacation, and in the middle of packing, rumors flew concerning evacuations and meltdowns. What is the danger? Is it coming this way? How much time do we have? Do we have to leave? What do we take? Hastily, things were gathered and stored by the front door, ready for flight. The evacuation order never came, and Pam and her family left on vacation, while all the eyes of the world were nervously watching their home state. They wondered whether they would ever be able to return, and whether those left behind would be safe. Obviously, they were.

More recently, after the tsunami hit Japan, many people were not allowed to return to their houses if they were within 24 miles of Fukushima, and they remain excluded at this writing. Today, there are many nuclear and other hazardous facilities located in heavily populated areas, and they are often relatively exposed. The Indian Point nuclear complex in New York is located within 50 miles of 8% of the US population, just 24 miles north of New York City. Here two operating nuclear-power plants have accumulated enormous stockpiles of highly radioactive waste in facilities that were not designed to withstand events of the kind that sometimes occur. If a disaster would strike around a nuclear plant near you, the possibility of your not returning is significant.

FIRE

The most common air-related emergency is *fire*, and most fire deaths come from smoke inhalation rather than from burning. Today's building materials are rich in complex toxic chemicals like formaldehyde—AKA embalming fluid—which are inside composition boards and most carpeting and furniture. When such materials smolder or burn, these toxic chemicals are released, and they can burn out your lungs and kill you quickly. Not only that, but with our modern houses built with so many inflammable materials, it can take less than 10 minutes to burn down. Older houses usually take longer.

In the event of a fire, hot smoke rises, so get on the floor and seek the cooler air which may be breathable. However, watch out for ground-hugging, foul-smelling, discolored air, which may be toxic chemicals. Find the breathable air, below the smoke and above the heavy chemical fumes. If you have any way to wet your clothes, and bandana, do so, including urination. Cover your nose and mouth with your wet bandana. Make your way down and away from the heat source. Open no door that feels hot; just seek another way out.

Rural Fire Protection

Anyone who observed the news coverage of wild fires will have noticed that the occasional house that survived the direct onslaught of wildfire had two characteristics—a metal roof and cleared land around the house. FEMA has a good checklist for rural fire protection.[1]

TIP
IF YOU LIVE IN A FIRE-THREATENED AREA, CLEAR BRUSH FOR AT LEAST 30 FEET AROUND YOUR BUILDING, AND BUILD ONLY WITH METAL ROOFS.

Smoke Detectors

Ninety percent of the time, when a person dies from fire, smoke detectors are absent, disabled, or dead.

TIP
ALWAYS HAVE A WORKING SMOKE DETECTOR.

Smoke detectors are essential, but know that children tend to sleep through standard smoke alarms for close to three minutes, which could be deadly.[2] Dr. Gary Smith, a researcher at Ohio's Nationwide Children's Hospital has studied smoke detectors and sleeping children for years, and he concludes that children are "biologically different than adults, and that's absolutely critical for us to understand when we're trying to prevent injury and death among children.... Children spend more time in deep sleep than adults do, and that's why it's harder for them to awaken in the case of an emergency."

---

1. http://tinyurl.com/FEMARuralFireSafety
2. http://tinyurl.com/KidsSleepThru

The National Institutes of Health conducted a study[1] comparing personalized parent-voice smoke alarms with conventional residential tone smoke alarms, and found that 96% of the 24 children tested awakened to the parent-voice alarm but only 58% awoke to the tone alarm.

TIP

DO NOT DEPEND UPON CONVENTIONAL RESIDENTIAL TONE SMOKE ALARMS TO WAKE CHILDREN. USE A PERSONALIZED PARENT-VOICE SMOKE ALARM.

Amazon carries a KidSmart Vocal Smoke Alarm Detector[2] for about $60, which is more than a conventional smoke alarm, but price should not be an obstacle when a child's safety rides in the balance.

There are two main types of smoke-detection technology—photoelectric and ionizing. Photoelectric alarms are faster to detect smoldering fires. In a test[3] carried out in Ohio, smoldering furniture was detected by photoelectric alarms 4.5 minutes into the test, while the first ionizing alarm went off 9.2 minutes later, when the sofa burst into flames. Most homes, however, use ionization alarms, which are faster to detect fast-burning fires, but can lead to false alarms like burning toast, for example, which leads some people to disable the alarm just to shut it up. If they forget to reset it later, people can die.

TIP

**RAGS DAMP WITH LINSEED OIL CAN GRADUALLY WARM AND BURST INTO FLAMES THROUGH SPONTANEOUS COMBUSTION.
PLACE USED OIL-SOAKED RAGS IN AN OLD PAINT BUCKET,
FILL IT WITH WATER, AND RESEAL IT. ONLY THEN IS IT SAFE TO DISCARD.**

When you are fleeing a fire, you may not have time to find your *Go Pack* (page 145), unless you have it already in the car or on the way out. Just get out alive. There is no need to plan for 72 hours of survival if you are dead from breathing bad air.

TIP

MAP OUT AN ESCAPE PLAN IN ADVANCE AND MAKE SURE THAT EACH ADULT HAS A DESIGNATED CHILD TO WAKE UP IN A REAL FIRE.

FIRE PREVENTION

FEMA was established to assist the American people during emergencies. Their material online is clear and authoritative, and we will not duplicate it here. Please refer to the

---

1. http://tinyurl.com/NIHalarmStudy
2. http://tinyurl.com/ParentsVoice
3. http://tinyurl.com/DetectorsTested

web site of FEMA's US Fire Administration,[1] where you can see detailed recommendations on a wide variety of fire-prevention and safety topics, including those in this table.

Fire Prevention Topics at FEMA	
Arson & Youth Firesetter Awareness	High-Rise Fire Safety
Bedroom Fire Safety	Holiday and Seasonal Fire Safety
Candle Fire Safety	Home Heating
Cooking Fire Safety	Fireplace Fire Safety
Earthquakes and Fire Safety	Residential Fire Sprinklers
Electrical Fire Safety	Rural Fire Safety
Escape Planning	Smoke Alarms
Fire Extinguishers	Smoking Fire Safety
Hazardous Materials Fire Safety	Wildfires

WARNING SIGNS OF DANGEROUS AIR

- Dead, dying or affected animals or people
- Discolored air in low-lying areas
- People fleeing
- Oily film or droplets on exposed surfaces
- Strange odors

TIP
STAY ALERT: EARLY DETECTION OF DANGER ENHANCES SURVIVAL.

In any air-related emergency, it will be essential to know two things: where is the wind coming from, and how fast is it moving? Perhaps you can get this information from your smart phone, or your local forecast. If not, you'll have to do it manually.

FINDING THE SPEED OF THE WIND

Look for a flag or windsock. With no wind, all flags are slack, but normal-sized ones stand out from the pole at about 12 mph. Practice gauging the wind speed by the degree to which the flags stand out from the pole. You might think about putting up a flagpole now, and not just to be patriotic.

---

1. http://tinyurl.com/FEMAFireSafety

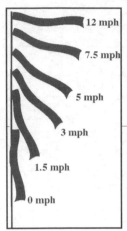

Be aware, however, that above 12 mph, this "gauge" provides little useful information. If you are in a danger area, you might consider buying an anemometer and wind vane, because the information would be good to have quickly and reliably.

FINDING THE DIRECTION OF THE WIND

If you are outside, watch a flag, or get to where the wind is not deflected by buildings. Wet your finger and raise it. The cooler side of your finger is the direction the wind is coming *from*.

From inside a building, look outside for flags, trees, blowing papers, *etc.*, but do not be misled by local deflections and whirlwinds, which are especially prominent within tall buildings.

Use your compass to read the *bearing* of the wind, *i.e.*, the degrees clockwise from North, and write it down (page 153), because you may need it to make a good decision about whether you need to go, and if so, which direction you should go.

Full directions on how to evacuate are on page 34.

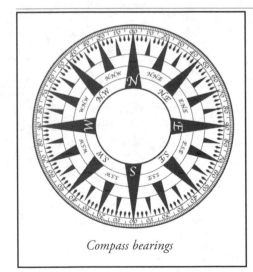

Compass bearings

ESCAPING FROM A PLUME

Evacuating from an on-coming threat is not an exact science. In the fall of 1999, Hurricane Floyd came roaring out of the Atlantic Ocean right toward Brian's sister in Myrtle Beach, S.C. Brian's friend offered to put her up in Durham, out of harm's way, but his sister insisted on toughing it out.

As it happened, Floyd turned northwest, missed Myrtle Beach, and clobbered Durham, felling a big oak tree on the very house his sister would have stayed in.

Weather phenomena are fickle. In the 1980 major eruption of Mt. St. Helens, the plume moved mainly east due to the prevailing winds. However, on subsequent eruptions, the plume moved in several directions at once, depending on where ash entered various layers of the atmosphere and which direction the wind was blowing at that particular elevation. The weather people became quite adept at advising citizens as to when ash would arrive in local towns and cities.

Radioactive Smoke Plume from Fukushima.

The radioactive plume from Fukushima was also quite variable and unpredictable from day to day. Usually, however, it is the heavy ground-level plumes that are both most dangerous and yet most predictable. On April 17, 2013, a chemical plant in West, Tex., exploded, nearly leveling the town, killing 14, injuring 200 and damaging 75 homes. A plume of hot, toxic gas arose from the event, but it rose high into the sky, requiring no plume-related evacuation.

The lesson is clear—know what hazards are in your area and make a mental note as to what your response would be if danger suddenly materialized.

West, Texas
Photo credit: AP

If a toxic plume of nasty business is spilling into your air shed, you will need to find out whether you need to evacuate, and if so, in what direction and by what time. If you are told to evacuate by authorities, then do so. If you are on your own, you will need to find out the direction and distance to the threatening event. To do so, follow these steps:

Pagami Creek fire 11/10/11 engulfed 90,000 acres in one day. Credit: MN Public Radio

HOW TO EVACUATE

1. Find out if you have to go

- No given means of communication can be guaranteed to work during an emergency, so tune into whatever news you can find, with your smart phone, battery-powered radio or vehicle radio, and follow official instructions. Write down the time the event occurred using the Evacuation Worksheet on page 153.

- In the absence of official guidance, locate yourself and the event on a good local map. Draw a line between them, and, using the scale, write down the distance of the event from you, in miles.

- Determine and write down the bearing of the line between you and the event in degrees clockwise from north. This will be a number between 0° (North) and 360° (North again, all the way around the compass). Find out the current direction of the wind, and write down the bearing of the source of the wind in degrees clockwise from north.

- If the two bearings are within 15° of each other, you are likely to be in the current path of the plume and will probably need to evacuate, unless the plume is hot and rising. If the two bearings are more than 15° apart, or the plume is hot and rising, you are likely to be out of the expected path of the plume and can stay put.

2. Find out how much time you have

- Estimate the speed of the wind. Write it down in miles per hour.

- Divide the distance to the event by the wind speed to get hours.

- Add this to the time you think the event occurred. This is the time when the plume can be expected to arrive—the time by which you must be gone.

3. Determine the direction to go

- Point a hand in the direction of the event. Name it "Hand A."

- Point the other hand into the wind. Name it "Hand B."

- Swing Hand A towards Hand B until it touches.

- Swing Hand B away to form a 90° (right) angle with Hand A.

Travel in the direction that Hand B points. This will be perpendicular to the wind direction, away from danger. Practice this, so that memory resides in your muscles, not just your brain. Take your portable Stash (see page 148) and go now with confidence to your preplanned rendezvous in that direction.

Table 1. Simplified Evacuation

Hot plumes that you can see rising usually require no evacuation, but radioactive plumes can be invisible, so treat them like cold plumes.

Determine the **direction** of the event (page 32).

With your first hand point in the direction of the **Event**.

With the second hand point into the **Wind**.

If there is **more than a fist** at arm's length between your two arms, you probably do **not** need to evacuate.

If your arms are **a fist or less apart**, swing your first arm to point upwind.

Swing your second arm away to form a **right angle** (90°) with the wind direction.

Evacuate in the direction that your second arm points, that is, away from the event and cross-wind.

(See "Evacuation Worksheet" on page 153)

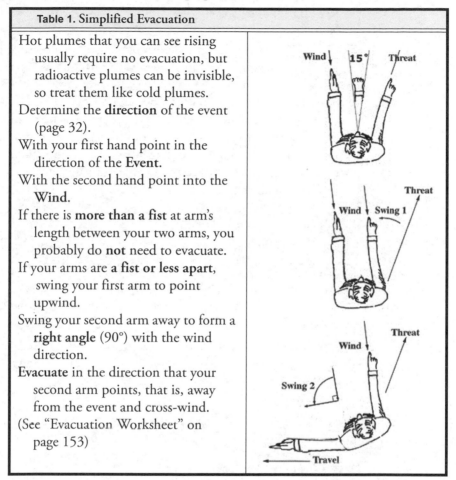

TIP
KEEP CURRENT PRINTED MAPS OF YOUR REGION AT HAND.
AMAZINGLY, THEY WORK WHEN YOUR POWER IS OUT,
WHEN YOUR CELL PHONE SERVICE IS ABSENT,
AND WHEN YOUR BATTERIES ARE DEAD!

Four Scenarios

AWAY FROM HOME, WITHOUT A VEHICLE

- Immediately wet your bandana or handkerchief and cover your nose and mouth with it.

- If you cannot walk immediately out of the affected area, then go inside and upstairs if possible, because bad air tends to flow downwards, following the local air-shed contours, like airy rivers. Seal yourself in a closed space as best you can.

Where to meet: See page 153.

- If you can walk out of danger, then do so at a steady pace in a cross-wind direction as above and proceed to the agreed-upon meeting place. When you have arrived at your site, do not endanger yourself by waiting too long for others. They may never arrive. If nasty air is on the way, save yourself and move out of its way. Leave a note, if possible, or if cell phones are working advise your companions what the situation is at your designated meet-up area and tell them where you are going.

AWAY FROM HOME, IN YOUR VEHICLE

- Immediately close all your windows and turn off your ventilation system. Wet and apply your bandana to your nose and mouth.

- Do not open any doors until you are out of danger. Listen to the radio or your smart phone to determine the source and nature of the danger.

- Refer to your road maps or GPS and determine the shortest primary and alternate routes that take you out of danger, traveling away from danger at right angles to the wind when possible, as discussed above.

- Drive carefully to the nearest agreed-upon rendezvous in the direction you are traveling. If you can't stay, leave a note, if possible.

STUCK AT HOME, WITH NASTY AIR OUTSIDE

- Immediately wet and apply your bandana to your nose and mouth.

- Close all windows and doors.

- Turn off the heating and ventilation system. To do: find where you can power down the HVAC system.

- Stuff newspapers or cloth under doors, or tape them with duct tape from your Stash.

- Then get into your *safehaven room* (see below), close the door, and put a water-soaked towel over the bottom crack. Contact your loved ones and wait it out. The safehaven is a good storage place for books, toys and games for diversion.

Safehaven Room

- As soon as possible, select a safehaven room in your home, ideally a
[...] upstairs room, with access to a toilet and telephone. If
[...] bucket with a tight lid,
[...] fort.

- St[...] , as they leak

- T[...] hin the room

If sever[...]
will eventua[...]
without lett[...]
taminants g[...]
with any luc[...] 4 hours. Don't
squander yo[...] vely early, and
once you ar[...]

for purchases made by check less than 7 days prior to the date of return, (ii) when a gift receipt is presented within 60 days of purchase, (iii) for textbooks, or (iv) for products purchased at Barnes & Noble College Booksellers that are listed for sale in the Barnes & Noble Booksellers inventory management system.

Opened music CDs/DVDs/audio books may not be returned, and can be exchanged only for the same title and only if defective. NOOKs purchased from other retailers or sellers are returnable only to the retailer or seller from which they are purchased, pursuant to such retailer's or seller's return policy. Magazines, newspapers, eBooks, digital downloads, and used books are not returnable or exchangeable. Defective NOOKs may be exchanged at the store in accordance with the applicable warranty.

Returns or exchanges will not be permitted (i) after 14 days or without receipt or (ii) for product not carried by Barnes & Noble or Barnes & Noble.com.

Policy on receipt may appear in two sections.

> How much water?
> See page 40.

It's you[...] sks, rubber suits
or stored-ai[...] nsive, and can
only be used for a short whi[...] [...] n this vein,
including waterproof clothing, boots, *etc.*, should be stored in your safehaven room. Always organize and use what you already have.

It might be wise to locate the stay-at-home portion of your *Stash* in the safehaven room. Alternatively, you might store such items in a storm shelter in the basement, or a central location in the house that is selected more for its ability to survive high winds than to keep out toxic air.

When you create a safehaven room or storm shelter, be sure to notify family members that you have a shelter, so that in case of an emergency, people will know to look for you there.

EVACUATED FROM HOME

> Portable Stash:
> See page 148.
>
> Blank list:
> See page 156.

- Evacuate as planned, selecting the rendezvous that lies in the evacuation direction, as discussed above, unless otherwise directed by authorities.

- Load your people and your portable Stash into your vehicle and move out. Do not forget the medications in the freezer, or other vital items deliberately stored elsewhere.

- You may want to copy and use the blank list to remind whomever is loading the Stash into the vehicle what other items to remember to get, and where they are located.

- Drive carefully and deliberately, and with confidence. You have time because you were prepared.

- Keep ventilation off and windows closed. Being able to evacuate quickly will help you avoid massive traffic jams.

- Using pre-scouted alternate routes may help you avoid getting stuck in traffic jams.

- Meet any others at the pre-arranged meeting location (page 153), if possible. Once assembled, travel out and upwind of the danger area and use your Stash to survive until it is clear what to do.

DUSK MASKS AND RESPIRATORS

In your *Go Pack* should be some N95 NIOSH-rated fiber face masks to cover your nose and mouth. Such devices, available for a few dollars in home-improvement stores, filter out 95% of the particles from the air breathed. They are commonly available online for under a dollar apiece, in packages of 20.[1]

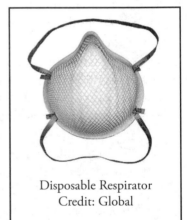

Disposable Respirator
Credit: Global

Such masks cannot do much against chemical agents, and they cannot prevent exposure to bioterrorism agents like anthrax, but they will reduce the risk. While they are not as effective as industrial gas masks with special filters for known agents, it is unlikely that you could have the right gas mask on your face before you needed it, and such devices restrict breathing, which is hazardous in itself. So equip yourself with N95 masks and swimming goggles for your eyes, and you will be much better off than if you don't.

TIP
STAY IN DAILY TOUCH WITH YOUR WEATHER PATTERNS
VIA SMART PHONE, WEATHER RADIO, TV OR THE INTERNET.
ALWAYS KNOW WHICH WAY TO TRAVEL AND WHY.

---

1. http://tinyurl.com/DisposableRespirators

7

Water

EVERYTHING YOU NEED TO KNOW, YOU LEARNED FROM NOAH'S ARK...
YOU CAN'T LIVE WITHOUT IT, BUT WATER IS NOT ALWAYS YOUR FRIEND.

In 2002, maps of municipal public water systems and dams were found in the living quarters of terrorists who were planning attacks on the US. On first glance, municipal water contamination seems like a plausible terrorist strategy, but a closer look at the ease with which water supplies dilute any contaminants placed in them and the huge quantities of poisons needed, one quickly concludes that this route is relatively improbable. Whether or not such attacks remain a matter of concern, it is clear that safely drinkable (potable) water is one of the most critical needs of the human body, so it is good to know how to find, purify, and store water, and how to evacuate from a flood or burst dam.

"Those who saw it coming described it as a rolling hill of debris about 40 feet high and a half a mile wide. But most only heard the thunderous rumble as it swept into the city...."[1]

The flood-soaked earthen dam that destroyed Johnstown, Penn., May 31, 1899, is instructive. 2209 people died. After the water fell, oil tanks leaked and the debris piles burned, killing more people. Today's dams are safer, but many are earthen and in disrepair, due to budget constraints. On July 15, 1982, the earthen Lawn Lake Dam in Rocky Mountain National Park suddenly released 220 million gallons of water, killing three campers and causing $31 million in damage to the town of Estes Park, Colo., and other downstream areas.

A dam is more likely to be a terrorist target if it is a hydroelectric dam, because of the double threat to both downstream populations and power supply, so be aware of what is upstream from you.

ESCAPING A BURST DAM

If you live where your elevation is below that of an upstream dam that is less than 100 river miles away, it would be prudent to be ready to permanently evacuate at a moment's notice. The Johnstown wall of flood water moved at 40

---

1. http://tinyurl.com/JohnstownFloodInfo

mph, so you will not have much time. This is another time when parking your vehicle in the direction you'll be going can save precious moments. If you get in the habit of doing this, it becomes second nature. In today's work of instant connection, it is likely that you'll hear of such a disaster coming your way, unless you are camping in an area without a cell-phone signal.

If you might get trapped in your attic with water rising outside, as was common during Katrina, store some water there in jugs (plastic, if freezing is possible), some emergency rations, and the key escape element—an axe.

WHAT TO KNOW ABOUT WATER

- Like the Earth, our body is 70% water by weight, and water lost through sweating or normal body functions must be replaced.
- The body requires a minimum of four quarts of water per day, increasing to several gallons for strenuous work on a hot day.
- Water helps maintain the body's temperature and is required for digestion and most other human functions.
- If your body's fluid drops by 2 quarts (or 2.5% of body weight), your body's efficiency drops by 25%.
- A fluid loss of 25% of body weight is usually fatal.
- Smoking, drinking alcohol and eating salty foods increase the need for water.

As a society, we have not only become mostly dependent on bottled water, but also water from our taps. If the flow should stop, you'll need to be prepared and creative. Living in the country where water from the well depends on electricity to run the pump, we personally learned to store water and keep a generator ready at all times in case of a power outage. Currently we have enough water stored in bottles to carry us through a week, if we use it sparingly and not for washing. We also have four rain-collecting barrels that we use for watering plants. If there were no fuel for the generator, and we had not received rain for a while, we would be hauling and purifying water from the nearby creek. Know where your nearest wild water is and how to treat it. (See page 41.)

HOW MUCH WILL YOU NEED?

The US Army recommends the following water consumption for soldiers: "A normally active person should take in at least four quarts of water each day, doubling that for hot environments and intense physical activity. Children, nursing mothers and ill people will need more." In your *Stash* (page 148) store one gallon of water per person per day (two quarts for drinking, two quarts for food preparation/sanitation), and even more if you have room.

WHEN WATER IS SHORT

- Find cool shade and just sit. In the south, it is sometimes said, "Why stand in the sun when you can sit in the shade?"
- Minimize your water intake by drinking slowly and in sips, which extends the time your water will last.
- Eat less fats and proteins, as they need more water to digest.
- Suck on a button or pebble to stimulate your saliva.
- Most people can survive three to five days without any water.

TIP
CHEWING GUM ALLEVIATES THIRST, AIDS IN DIGESTION,
AND IS EASILY STORED.

COLLECTING RAINWATER

The ideal way to collect rainwater is from a roof. The larger the roof, the more rainwater will be collected. Our two 40-gallon rain barrels fill up in minutes during a good storm. A spigot on each one makes it convenient for filling watering cans. Rain barrels with screens and spigots can often be found for sale for under $100.00.[1] Do not drink this water unless you treat it (see page 41).

Plastic rain barrels may crack and leak with age. Marine-grade epoxy can be used to repair the leaks, even when they are still wet. Tap Plastics, *e.g.*, has a good variety of marine-grade epoxy products.[2]

TIP
WHEN COLLECTING RAINWATER THAT WILL SIT OUTSIDE,
EITHER KEEP IT TIGHTLY COVERED OR REGULARLY ADD SOME OIL
(EVEN HOUSEHOLD COOKING OIL) TO THE WATER
TO PREVENT MOSQUITOES FROM BREEDING.

If you live in the city, you can still collect water off of the roof in barrels that are connected to your rain spouts. Before a crisis, seek an agreement with your building neighbors on how to allocate, preserve and use this water.

PRESERVING AND PURIFYING WATER

Only 5% of the surface water on our planet is safely drinkable (potable), so even the remotest water source may need to be treated before being drunk. Water-purification tablets are inexpensive, small and indispensable in a water

---

1. http://tinyurl.com/RainBarrelSource
2. http://tinyurl.com/FixBarrelLeaks

emergency. Keep some in your *Go Pack* and in your portable *Stash*. You can also purchase iodine tablets to kill most of the germs found in water, except *Cryptosporidium*, which causes diarrhea. The iodine tablets are often sold with "chasers" that take away the iodine taste after the germs have been disabled. Read the directions carefully on the package. For instance, iodine tablets lose their potency a few months after the bottle is opened. These should be replaced annually. A good non-electric water filter does make better-tasting water than pills, but it is also bigger and more expensive.[1]

You can make an inexpensive but temporary water filter from common materials. Cut the bottom out of a large soda bottle, clean it, invert it and put cotton batting in its mouth. Cover that with washed, crushed charcoal, perhaps from your campfire. Cover that with a layer of fine sand, then coarser sand, then fine gravel then coarser gravel, then a coffee filter if you have one. Water poured in the top drips out the bottom as filtered water, cleaner, but not guaranteed to be safe.[2] A commercial version that captures bacteria, parasites, herbicides, pesticides, solvents, nitrates, nitrites, lead, mercury, chlorine, VOCs, and even fluoride is available from Berkey for under $300.[3]

TIP

**HAVING WATER IS A HIGHER PRIORITY
THAN HAVING CHEMICAL-FREE WATER.**

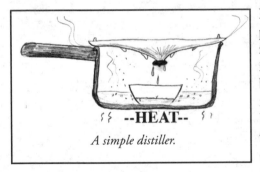

A simple distiller.

Boiling water is the safest way to purify it, but boiling water away from your stove can be challenging. Bring water to a full rolling boil (keep the lid on to avoid too much evaporation), and let it cool before drinking. Boiled or stored water will taste better if you return oxygen to it by pouring it back and forth between two containers.

Know where your water comes from, and periodically check its safety, whatever its source. Your local government agencies can point you in the right direction to get your water tested. In these changing times, we can't always assume that our drinking water is safe.

---

1. http://tinyurl.com/PortableWaterPurifier
2. diagram: Carr, p. 54.
3. http://tinyurl.com/GravityWaterFilter

DISTILLING

If your water is contaminated with chemicals, the *only* way to purify it is through distilling. You'll need two containers—one to boil the water, with an inverted lid on it, and a second to be placed under the lid to catch the distilled drips. Drinking distilled water all the time is not healthy. It will pull minerals from your body if you drink too much too often.

STORING WATER

Preserve water before storing it long-term, so that nothing grows in it. Liquid bleach, containing 5.25% sodium hypochlorite and no soap, is good. Add four drops per quart of water (or two scant teaspoons per 10 gallons), and stir. Seal your water containers tightly, label and date them, and store them in a cool, dark place. Too much bleach will make the water taste awful.

You can store your water in thoroughly washed, clear-plastic, fiberglass or enamel-lined metal containers. Never use a container that has held toxic substances, because tiny amounts will leach out from the container's pores. Soft-drink containers are good for limited times. You can also purchase food-grade plastic buckets or drums. Do not use translucent plastic milk jugs—they will leak in a few months.

Use and replace stored water on a regular rotation of a few months time to keep it fresh. The old water can be used to water plants, wash dishes, flush toilets and other uses.

About BPA and plastic water bottles

Bisphenol A (BPA) is in many food and liquid containers. The CDC has found BPA in the urine of 93% of Americans sampled. In 2008, Canada banned BPA in polycarbonate baby bottles due to safety concerns.

BPA plastics

Since the Canadian ban, most responsible manufacturers of plastic beverage containers have switched to the use of other materials.

Some guidelines on safely using plastics that may contain BPA:

- Plastic containers with recycle codes 3 or 7 may be made with BPA.
- Outside of emergencies, reduce your intake of canned foods, because the interior lining often contains BPA.
- When possible, use glass, porcelain or stainless steel containers, particularly for hot food or liquids.

- Use BPA-free baby bottles. Parents Magazine has a list of 15 BPA-free baby bottles and sippy cups.[1]
- Do not microwave food containers made of polycarbonate, which is strong and durable, but breaks down fin heat, releasing BPA.

FINDING WATER

We mentioned how in recent earthquakes, people have survived for extended periods of time because they were trapped in or under bathrooms or kitchens, where broken pipes or water heaters dribbled enough water for them to suck up. Be alert for opportunities.

In looking for water in nature remember that water moves towards the lowest level, where, if it cannot find a place to flow to, it will form a pool, swamp, bog, or, in extreme conditions, a temporary or permanent pond. Many cities were historically located next to rivers or lakes, thereby providing a major water source, but such water needs to be purified. Many rivers on our planet are toxic and should not be swum in, much less drunk without purification.

If it rains, collect whatever you can. After a rain, you'll find water that has collected in flower pots, tables, pools, gullies and behind rocks. Even roadside bottles, cans, bags and cups often contain fluids that can be solar-distilled in desperate times (see page 46). You must prioritize your actions if you wish to survive. It is unwise, for example, to choose to die of dehydration rather than consume roadside water sources.

If you live in a city with local parks where vegetation is blooming, follow the natural water flows. If you're in the country, observe the natural water flows that are visible on the sides of hills and mountains or in fields and lawns. Trees and shrubs are denser where the water flow is greater, so it will be greener. When you find these areas, dig down a couple of feet and allow it to settle. Dry stream or creek beds may still have water below the surface—dig down until you reach moisture.

In a muddy, damp area, you can dig a hole up to two feet in diameter. Wait until the water seeps into the hole. Purify it and use it. If you live in a sandy area, wet sand can be put into your bandana or other fine cloth, pressed or wrung out into a container, and then purified. Water taken from the soil or sand may be cloudy. You can either allow it to settle or filter it through another piece of fine cloth.

If you are in the woods and find a spring, it is most likely safe and one of the best waters you can drink since it is mature and mineral-rich, which is

---

1. http://tinyurl.com/BabyBottlesNoBPA

good for you. To confirm it is a spring, it will bubble up directly from the ground and will be crystal clear. If you have any doubts, boil or purify it.

Dew collects most mornings on plants and can even be collected by gently shaking the leaves over the plastic sheet or trash bag that should be in your *Go Pack*. Another method of collecting moisture from plants is to cover a leafy plant with your plastic trash bag. Dig a shallow hole just next to the plant, trying not to disturb too many roots. Cover the plant with the bag, which you press down into the adjacent hole.

Secure the bag with rocks or whatever you have available. The water that is given off by the plant will condense on the inside of the bag, slowly dripping and dribbling down into the hole, where it will pool. The plant will continue absorbing water with its roots and evaporating it into the bag, where it condenses and runs into the plastic-lined hole. This method will work for a few days. If it is important to preserve the plant, be careful not to burn it by covering it on hot, sunny days, as the plant will overheat and die.

If you live in desert areas, again watch nature. Follow the flight of birds at dawn or sunset, as they will often circle water holes (this does not include birds of prey, who use their victims as a source of fluid and look for water less frequently). Animals will gravitate to water, as will flying insects. Follow dry river beds up to their source if you can, where you may still discover a trickle of water. Also look for cottonwood trees in arid regions, as they tend to grow where there is water.

Look for water around vegetation at the base of cliffs. Also the pulp of some cacti can be ground into a watery mash.

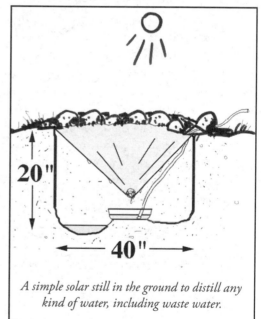

A simple solar still in the ground to distill any kind of water, including waste water.

We've already mentioned the importance of obtaining a good book about your local plants, if you don't know yours already. Along the coastlines find a sand depression at least 100 feet from the shore and dig a shallow hole. Rainwater collects on the top of saltwater behind the dunes. Do not go too deep, as you will soon reach brackish water, which is unpalatable. Again, you can also strain water from wet sand and purify before consuming.

MAKING A SOLAR STILL

We suggest you keep a small utility shovel, a clear sheet of 1-mil plastic at least 6' square in your *Go Pack* for various uses, such as a solar still. You'll also need a small container to place on the bottom and a 4' to 6' clear plastic tube to use as a straw.

Dig a hole about 40" wide with steep sides about 20" deep. To increase the amount of water collected, dig another smaller hole next to the collecting container that is about 12" wide and 4" to 6" deep. You can place waste fluids in it, including urine, plant material, and any scrounged water. Distilling will purify the waste water. Place a container in the middle of the bottom of the big hole. In your *Go Pack* you should have six feet of plastic tubing, wrapped with some all-purpose duct tape. So you don't have to dismantle the still and stop production, tape the plastic "straw" to the container with the duct tape and lead it up the side of the hole, securing it and keeping it clean so you can sip from it when distilled water appears.

Place the plastic sheeting over the hole and secure it around the edges with rocks and soil from the hole. Place a rock in the center of the plastic, heavy enough to pull the plastic down into a cone shape so that it reaches about 4" above the container. It should not be touching any soil on the sides.

Within a few hours, the temperature inside will have heated up enough to begin forming condensation on the cooler plastic sheeting. This water will dribble down along the sheeting into the container, yielding from one to three quarts per day in temperate regions and perhaps a quart of water per day in the desert. It is better to create a second small still than to make a larger one. If it rains, the plastic sheeting will collect drinking water, but be sure to keep scooping it so it does not pull everything into the hole.

Four Scenarios

AWAY FROM HOME, WITHOUT A VEHICLE

Carry at least a quart of water with you wherever you go. By keeping a shoulder-slung water bottle harness with you, you can always stay hydrated.

AWAY FROM HOME, IN YOUR VEHICLE

Keep water in your vehicle for emergencies, preferably two quarts per person, kept fresh. Although glass does not leach PBAs into the water, use glass only when you expect your vehicle not to freeze, and keep clear glass bottles of water out of direct sunlight, because they can act like magnifying glasses and create fires.

Escaping your Vehicle in a Flood

If perchance your vehicle is heading for deep water, open your window immediately—it may be hard or impossible to open the window once it is under water, as an accident or water can short out power windows. Seconds matter. Do not depend upon some imaginary trapped air bubble. As soon as you hit the water, unlatch your seat belt and float out through your window. Tell passengers in the back seat to get unbuckled immediately and follow you out your window. Help them get out. Go over this drill before the issue unexpectedly arrives, *especially* if you live in a flood-prone area.

STUCK AT HOME, NO UTILITIES

> To Do List:
> Use page 156.

Know the location of your incoming water valve. If you hear reports of broken water lines or contaminated municipal water supplies, you must quickly shut this valve to stop contaminated water from entering your home. You will be stockpiling treated water in your home, which you should use only for drinking. You can also use the water in your hot-water tank, in your plumbing, in ice cubes, and in the toilet tanks, which is only tap water. Do not use water from the toilet bowl, which is likely to be contaminated.

- To use the water in pipes, let air into the pipes by opening the highest faucet in your house, then drain water from the lowest one.

- To use the water in your hot-water tank, turn off the electricity or gas, open a hot-water faucet, then open the drain at the bottom of the tank. Do not turn the gas or electricity back on when the tank is empty, or it will burn out.

- To use a water bed to store water, drain it annually and refill it with fresh water containing two oz. of bleach per 120 gal. It may hold 400 gallons or so, which can still be used for washing or to flush toilets, even if you do not plan for its use as potable water.

EVACUATED FROM HOME

In your *Stash* and *Go Pack* you will have water-purification tablets. In cold climates, pipes may freeze and burst without heat, so before leaving, shut off the water and drain the pipes *if* you have time. Take as much stored water with you as you can easily manage, which should be readily available.

8

Temperature

EVERYTHING YOU NEED TO KNOW, YOU LEARNED FROM NOAH'S ARK...
THE ARK WAS BUILT BY AMATEURS, THE TITANIC BY PROFESSIONALS.

Hypothermia
and heat stroke:
See page 96.

Smoke Detectors:
See page 29.

In recent years, wildfires have ravaged the American west, due to extended drought, and common sense would suggest that this "reaction" has its roots in the reduction in moisture caused by deforestation of the Amazon rainforest. Our planet is getting smaller—what we do in one place can affect another place, even thousands of miles away. We are finding that we are all connected.

Even if you have a beautiful home with solid walls, an emergency can unexpectedly separate you from it, perhaps permanently. You may be stuck in a tunnel under a river, or your vehicle may become inoperable in the country, or your neighborhood may suddenly be an inferno. Knowing how to stay warm or cool is an important survival skill in each of these emergencies.

Staying Warm

Freezing weather can kill you faster than anything but asphyxiation. Hypothermia, where the internal body temperature falls to a point that causes organs to fail, can set in at temperatures as high as 50°F, when it is wet and windy.

We spoke to a not-so-old-timer, native to the hills of western North Carolina, who explained that as a child he had to haul all their water a good distance every day. To our surprise, he told us that folks in that rural area did not get electricity until about 1948. He remembered being able to see outside through the slats in the wall boards, and he told us that if he kept water in his glass by his bed at night, it was often frozen solid by morning. We surmise that they all had warm bed covers or bed warmers. He recalls that people didn't get colds as much then as they do today—that their bodies really did get used to the temperature. (This supports our theory that it may be the sudden *variations* in temperature and humidity from going in and out of climate-controlled buildings and vehicles that causes many of our health problems.)

Four Scenarios

AWAY FROM HOME, WITHOUT A VEHICLE

If there is any possibility that you could get stuck in the open without a vehicle, then please factor in survivability along with your style preferences when you dress. You may have to stay warm and walk far, so basic clothing and warm, comfortable shoes are important.

You will need to seek shelter with other humans. In an emergency most people are more than willing to help, and will often risk their own lives to do so. You may have information or skills that others may need and vice versa.

> *Pocket Set*:
> See page 15.

AWAY FROM HOME, IN YOUR VEHICLE

If you have followed the guidelines of this book, your vehicle will be equipped with a *Vehicle Box* and a *Go Pack* before leaving home. If your car is unable to move due to snow and ice, or you've had an accident, use the emergency space blanket in your *Go Pack* to hold in your body warmth. Keep a space

> *Vehicle Box*:
> See page 147.
> *Go Pack*:
> See page 145.

blanket in your car for each member of your family. You should also have there some old clothes, especially woolen socks, sweater and gloves. Wear all the clothing you can find, wrap yourself in the space blanket and stay in your vehicle until help arrives.

- Do not go for help in the snow— it can kill you. The only time it is wise to leave your vehicle is if you are sure of your surroundings and know you can walk to help.

- Call for help with your cell phone if you can.

- Run your engine's heater for 10 to 15 minutes every hour, which is a good reason to always keep your tank almost full. This will not only keep you warm, but it will also melt snow around you, making you more visible. While running the engine, crack a window in case your tail pipe is covered, which will prevent carbon monoxide fumes from entering the car.

- Your *Go Pack* should have in it some emergency food and space blankets to keep you warm. (See page 145.)

- In case you become stranded on a highway, keep your seat belt on, in case some other car runs into yours.

In warmer climates, if you're out of gas or your car is immobile, use your car for shade during the day and for warmth at night, and use your space blanket if you can't walk for help.

STUCK AT HOME, NO UTILITIES

If your home has a fireplace or woodstove, the only thing you'll need for warmth is good insulation and a dry wood supply. Keep enough wood on hand for several weeks of cold weather, if you have room, but stack most of it away from the house in case of a forest fire. Hardwoods like oak burn hotter and last longer than softwoods like pine, which can also let creosote build up in your chimney, which can cause chimney fires, the leading cause of burned-out cabins in the woods. An open fireplace draws more heat up the chimney than it provides, making outer rooms colder, so it is best to have an air-tight fireplace enclosure, preferably with a built-in heat exchanger that can operate via natural convection, even without power. If you don't have an insert, a fireplace will keep you warm—especially if you can close off the room and stay close.

Reminder: Most of us are accustomed to electric lights and furnaces that operate efficiently. When using candles, fireplaces, oil lamps, *etc.*, use the utmost caution. Train children to stay away from open flames, clean your chimney annually to avoid fires, keep combustible items away from heat sources, and be cautious.

If you live in a cold climate, you have probably experienced the beauty of life slowing down when the electric fails. As long as you have candles, oil lamps and some food stored, just get out the games and have some fun. In an extended emergency, electrical and battery-powered games will die, so keep some good old-fashioned card and board games around.

Propane heaters are an excellent short-term source of heat. Make sure you have an extra tank or two and use it wisely, as the price and availability of propane may fluctuate wildly during an extended emergency. Kerosene heaters also work, but they are more dangerous and they can smell bad and cause headaches for some people.

Windows lose heat rapidly at night. Close your curtains or blinds at night to keep out the cold. If you don't have curtains, you can cover them with blankets. If you have large, south-facing windows, even in winter you can warm your house with the sun. On dreary cold days, keeping most of the windows covered will retain heat, but most of us find that we need some natural light to keep up our spirits.

In parts of the world without central heat, houses are built with rooms that close off because it is efficient to heat the house one room at a time with a small heater. If the lights go out, you'll be doing the same thing. Since most of us live in modern open houses that do not have this kind of efficient construction, you may need to use blankets to close off rooms as well as cover windows.

If you can afford feather beds or down comforters, you will find them light and very warm. Some of the new synthetic-filled comforters are also very warm and more affordable. Flannel sheets also make a huge difference in warming your bed. Even without emergencies, if you turn the heat down at night, you'll still be toasty warm with these bed coverings. You may also find that your family will be a little healthier and, of course, your heating bill will be less.

The US Army Acclimatization Schedule allows for regular work duty after five days of acclimation to temperatures less than 105°F, and after six days of acclimation to temperatures above 105°F. In time we all adjust to the heat.

EVACUATED FROM HOME

Your *Go Pack* and your portable *Stash* will go with you in your vehicle, and should be properly equipped with tents, sleeping bags, clothing, footwear and other gear to keep you warm, especially if motels and hotels are not readily available. Check your gear periodically to make sure the lighters work and the matches are dry. Campfires keep your body warm

Go Pack: See page 145.
Stash: See page 148.

and your spirits up. They still touch something ancient in each of us.

And don't forget kindling. If you're camping in the rain, do not assume that you'll find dry twigs. Firesticks are manufactured kindling. Keep some in your *Stash*. You can also gather up small dry twigs in a box when you have them, and store the box with your *Stash*. Fire logs are too bulky and heavy to consider carrying with you. If you are out in the woods, gather up kindling and any dry logs you can use for burning. Twigs caught in branches will be drier than those on the ground.

Clothing

Functional clothes and footwear can make a huge difference. Most people know this, but too often we put fashion before function. When storing clothes in your *Go Pack*, obviously think function. It is easier to take off clothes when it is hot than it is to find warmer clothes when it is not, so for folks in colder climates, keeping warm clothes in your car is vital and you probably already practice this.

Keep a wool stocking cap in your *Stash*. Ten percent of your body heat can be lost through your head, not the 40 to 45% that has been believed for decades. The head surface is about 10% of your body mass, so experts now believe that this is the percentage of heat you would lose, but it varies slightly depending on your exercise level and depending on whether your head is the only uncovered part of your body. It is still a good idea to cover your head and ears in the cold.

TIP

ONLY 10% OF BODY HEAT IS LOST THROUGH THE HEAD.

Staying Cool

Pocket Set: See page 15.

Half of the 60,000 annual deaths in the US from natural disasters are caused by heat. See page 95 for treatment of heat stroke, heat exhaustion, and heat cramps.I

If you reside in desert areas, you are probably well aware of how to stay cool. In the daytime without a hat or covering for your body, you will need to find shade, and at night you'll need to have covering for warmth. You should have in your *Pocket Set* a bandana, which can serve as a head cover in case you don't have a broad rimmed hat with you.

STUCK AT HOME, NO UTILITIES

It is interesting that honey bees cool down their temperature by holding a droplet or two of nectar honey in the folds of their tongues. John Heinerman of the Anthropological Research Center of Salt Lake City did some experiments on human subjects on a hot July day. They discovered that chewing a small piece of honeycomb and keeping it in the mouth for as long as possible during periods of strenuous physical activity produced a drop in body temperature. You can get the same effect by putting some granulated honey in some gauze and chewing it occasionally.[1] It might be good to keep some of this wonder of the honey bees in your *Go Pack* and *Stash*, but well-sealed, as it is messy when it leaks.

Most windows gain heat rapidly in the summer sun. Without electricity there won't be any fans blowing, nor air conditioners cooling our homes and offices. Before almost everyone had air conditioning, people opened windows wide at night and closed windows and curtains during the day. This works, and houses usually stay relatively cool until late afternoon and early evening, when you can move outside until the house cools off again.

The house will remain cooler if you cook only in the early morning. If there is no electricity for cooking, you can barbecue or use a fire outside. If you

---

1. Heinerman, p. 220

are a city dweller, and can't build a fire somewhere, resort to your easy-to-eat foods that don't require cooking or need only heated water.

Try to use only 100% cotton sheets, light blankets, bed clothes and clothing that breathes, which will help keep you cooler. Stay calm and don't exert yourself until you have adjusted to the heat.

A wet bandana can be worn around your neck, over your face, or on your head as the need arises. Your carotid artery runs up the neck and transports a large amount of blood throughout the body. As it passes the cool bandana, the blood is cooled, which cools the rest of your body. Neck-cooler scarves,[1] when moistened for several minutes, will keep you cool for quite a while.

FEMA makes these suggestions:[2]

- When it is very hot, try to spend the hottest part of the day in air-conditioned buildings, or at least near water or in shade.

- Listen to NOAA Weather Radio for critical updates (see page 109).

- Never leave children or pets alone in closed vehicles.

- Avoid strenuous outdoor exertion during the warmest part of the day. Use a buddy system when working in extreme heat, and take frequent breaks.

- Dress in loose-fitting, lightweight, and light-colored clothes that cover as much skin as possible. Avoid dark colors because they absorb the sun's rays.

- Protect your face and head with a wide-brimmed hat, perhaps over a bandana to protect your neck from the sun.

- Eat well-balanced, light, and regular meals. Drink plenty of water, even without thirst. (See page 39.) Avoid caffeine and alcohol.

- Consult a doctor before increasing liquid intake if you have epilepsy, heart, kidney, or liver disease, are fluid-restricted or have fluid-retention issues.

- Check on family, friends, and neighbors without air conditioning.

- Stay calm. Getting excited makes you hotter.

TIP

TO FIND A NEARBY SHELTER FOR ANY REASON,
TEXT "SHELTER 12345" TO 4FEMA, WHERE 12345 IS YOUR ZIP CODE.

---

1. http://tinyurl.com/NeckCoolerScarf
2. http://tinyurl.com/PrepareForHeat

9

Food

EVERYTHING YOU NEED TO KNOW, YOU LEARNED FROM NOAH'S ARK...
TAKE WHAT YOU NEED WITH YOU.

Food-related issues are a concern in each of the four basic emergency situations we have outlined. Fortunately, it takes three to five weeks to starve to death, so food is the least of your immediate worries. In this chapter we are talking mostly about food that sustains your comfort and psychological well-being. Increasing economic uncertainty, unstable weather patterns, and inflation are causing food prices to skyrocket, so locking in food prices in the form of properly stored food is wise.

Four Scenarios

AWAY FROM HOME, WITHOUT A VEHICLE

Carry some cash with you at all times, in case you find a way to buy some food. Most of us don't carry much cash anymore because of debit cards, but card-based transactions may not work during emergencies. If you can find people, someone will probably share food with you. People are generally generous and compassionate, despite media coverage that exploits negativity. Learning how to identify and use edible wild plants could also come in handy some day.

AWAY FROM HOME, IN YOUR VEHICLE

Go Pack List:
See page 145.

Vehicle Box List:
page 147

It is recommended that you keep in your *Go Pack* some dried food, such as jerky, or military MREs,[1] which can be found in surplus stores or ordered via Internet sites. Costco and other big-box stores now offer online dozens of bulk dried food sets for emergencies, most for under $100.[2] More dried food can be kept in the *Vehicle Box*, but take care to keep any food items from being contaminated by oil or other engine-fluid containers

---

1. MREs = Meals, Ready to Eat
2. http://www.costco.com

you might be storing there. Make sure you have plenty of water ready before you eat dried food, because it will make you thirsty.

If you are a vegetarian, take extra care concerning what you stock. If you saw the film "Life of Pi," you will remember how long vegetarian Pi remained hungry before consuming fish. Survival trumps food preferences.

STUCK AT HOME, NO UTILITIES

The first line of food defense at home is to keep your refrigerator, freezer, and kitchen food cabinets well stocked, just as it is wise to keep your vehicle well fueled. It is recommended that you always keep your pantry supplied with the basics—eggs, milk, butter, cooking oil, vinegar, flour, sugar, baking powder and baking soda, corn starch, salt, black pepper and your favorite spices and herbs. You may have no warning before being stuck at home for a long time. In such cases, ample food is a real blessing, and cooking is a diverting activity.

If the power goes out, use the refrigerated food before it spoils, then use the frozen foods, minimizing the number and length of time the freezer door is opened. A full, well-insulated freezer will usually keep foods for at least three days. If there are still ice crystals in the center, the food should be safe to eat, but if it has an odor, throw it out. Thaw frozen foods you plan to eat in your refrigerator, thus helping to keep it cool. Once you've exhausted the perishable foods, move on to your stored and non-perishable items.

Long-term food storage.

Cooking food without utilities can be a hassle, but the Internet has stepped up to the challenge at sites like Costco,[1] MyFoodStorage,[2] Thrive Emergency Food,[3] Emergency Essentials,[4] The Survival Center,[5] and eFoods.com,[6] all of which have a wide variety of long-term food storage products for sale.

A recent innovation derived from the military allows us to have good, hot meals without using any electricity or fuel. MREs are the Meals Ready to Eat that the military issues to its soldiers. They are generally tasty and nutritious, have a shelf life of up to 10 years and can heat themselves. In standard MREs the unopened waterproof food packet is placed in a plastic bag, along with special powder and water. It is

1. http://tinyurl.com/CostcoEmergencyFood
2. http://tinyurl.com/SkinSoSoftChoices
3. http://www.thriveemergencyfoods.com
4. http://beprepared.com
5. http://tinyurl.com/Survival-Ctr-Food
6. http://www.efoodsdirect.com

propped up, and some minutes later the hot, pre-cooked food is ready. Heater meals are similar, but come in a box that heats itself. A pack of 12 MREs with heaters or Heater Meals can be purchased online for around $55 from websites such as Epicenter.[1] While such foods cost more than bulk foods, eating at most restaurants costs more than an MRE. At $6.50 per hot meal, this alternative has some advantages over more traditional ways to cook food during short-term emergencies. In particular, there is no need to procure cooking gear or haul it with you. During an emergency, your priority is to stay alive, so forget about whether or not the MREs are gourmet, organic or locally made.

Cooking with Fire

If you have a fireplace or wood stove, you might purchase some cast-iron cookware that can be placed on a grate in the fire or directly onto the wood stove. Cast-iron cookware can be found in many stores and garage sales. If you are thinking about getting a wood stove, consider a model with a flat top, so you can cook on it if you need to. You can purchase a cast-iron fry pan or a slow-cooking pot to simmer food all day.

TIP

**BE VERY CAREFUL WITH ANY OPEN-FLAMED COOKING,
ESPECIALLY WITH CHILDREN AROUND.
HAVE ONE OR MORE MULTI-USE FIRE EXTINGUISHERS AVAILABLE
(THE SMALL CANISTER, ABC TYPE),
AND MAKE SURE PEOPLE KNOW HOW TO USE THEM.**

Keep plenty of heavy-duty aluminum foil in your *Stash*. You'll be amazed at what you can put together inside foil and place in the coals of a fire—everything from meat to vegetables can be placed in foil with seasonings and a little oil if required, sealed up tightly and placed in a portion of the fire that will cook it without burning it. Also, remember that food can be cooked on sticks or rocks. Be creative and imaginative—you may surprise yourself. Remember, when life gives you lemons, make lemonade.

TIP

WHEN THE POWER IS OFF, THINK OF IT AS A CAMP-OUT.

A propane grill can become your kitchen stove. You can also heat food in chafing dishes and fondue pots, or on top of candle warmers, although it could take a while. Propane camp stoves with extra propane bottles are available from outdoor stores. These stores also carry a variety of small cooking units that use

---

1. http://theepicenter.com

small cans of gelled fuel like Sterno. You will not die from the lack of hot, tasty food, but we've certainly become accustomed to it, so it's good to be prepared to provide hot food, even during an emergency.

You will also need to think about what you will eat *on*. If you have ready access to water and fire, you'll be able to wash dishes. Otherwise, you may want to begin accumulating paper plates, bowls, cups and plastic utensils that can be used without the need for washing. You also have fingers.

Other items to stock: a metal grill for cooking meat, long barbecue utensils for working with fire, bottle openers, can openers and heavy-duty hot pads, which most of us have around.

THE HOME FOOD STASH

Thrive long-term food storage.

Your kitchen food may run out, and if the emergency is still on, you will need to use your *Stash*, where you are encouraged to store a variety of long-shelf-life food items, enough to last you and your family perhaps a month. When you are building your food *Stash*, designate a portion to be quickly loaded into your vehicle if you should need to be evacuated (see page 61), and keep the remainder, mainly heavier, bulkier items, for home use.

The Church of the Latter Day Saints encourages its faithful to stockpile emergency food and keep a current inventory list of what is in the food *Stash*. Make copies of the empty list

Blank list: See page 156.

and keep them and a pencil by the food *Stash* in order to update the list each time you add or delete something. Another copy of the list can be used when going to the store. Use your stored food on a periodic basis, and rotate it, using the oldest food first. Here is another place to get the children involved—have them retrieve an item from the *Stash*, mark the list and they'll become accustomed, along with you, to keeping it up to date. In addition, they will feel that they are making themselves useful by contributing to the family's needs.

It is best to store food in a place that is cool, dark and well ventilated. Store your food in airtight containers to preserve its freshness and to protect it from pests and dirt. Food purchased in bulk can be transferred to clean, dry, glass jars, plastic containers with tight-fitting lids, or labeled and dated freezer bags, which fit compactly into tight spaces. If the container is inadequate, you can ruin much stored food and waste a lot of money. Many bulk items come in airtight containers, or you can purchase this type of bucket separately.

Keeping your pantry full and stashing a month's food supply can be financially daunting, but keep the thought in mind that you are "building" a pantry. When you shop, begin buying pairs of storable items and put one away. Often grocery stores offer buy-one-get-one-free (BOGO) sales. Take advantage of this, and you'll be surprised how quickly it will accumulate.

We personally prefer to eat fresh, healthy foods that are free of preservatives and additives, but in setting up your *Stash,* stick to items that are not perishable and do not require refrigeration. Typically, such foods will have preservatives in them, but the large buckets of rice, beans, grains, *etc.,* will not, nor will the better freeze-dried foods. Again, when your life hangs in the balance, worrying about preservatives can be deferred to better times.

Suggestions for Stocking the Food Stash

The best approach is to store large amounts of staple foods along with a variety of canned and dried foods. Bulk quantities of salt and unprocessed wheat, corn, and beans are inexpensive and have nearly unlimited shelf life, but it takes more time to prepare and cook them. If necessary, you could survive for quite a while on small daily amounts of these staples. Bulk foods must be inspected periodically, and rotated in usage. Check the "FEMA Recommended Food Items" on page 154 for the federal government's recommendations.

Rice is a great staple to stock up on in great quantity, and it can be used in a variety of ways. Brown rice is more nutritious than white rice, but it requires longer cooking time, which must be considered if cooking is difficult. Bulk rice can be stored in freezer bags in smaller quantities that fit nicely into available spaces in your packs. American rice has been found to contain some arsenic, with white rice being six times more contaminated than brown rice[1] but again, in an emergency, your priority is staying alive.

Bulk grains will last longer than ground grains when storing for long-term use. If you store whole grains, you will need a hand-cranked grain mill from a health-food store, or from suppliers such as Emergency Essentials[2] or Cumberland General Store.[3] If you are caught without a grinder, you can make your own by filling a large can one inch deep with the whole grain you want to grind. Put the can on the ground between your feet and pound the grain with a pipe. Take turns with other family members. It's good exercise, too.

Unbleached or white all-purpose flour has a longer shelf life, but whole wheat is more nutritious. If you are allergic to wheat, you will already know

---

1. http://tinyurl.com/NIH-ArsenicRice
2. http://tinyurl.com/BulkGrains
3. http://tinyurl.com/CumberlandGeneral

about other flours such as oat, barley, spelt, millet, quinoa, rye or amaranth. These must be stored in air-tight containers.

Corn can be used either dried for slow cooking in soups and stews or canned for quick warm ups.

Beans and legumes are great, storable sources of protein, and they come in many varieties. You can stock them canned or dried and use them in stews, soups, salads or main dishes. Dried beans require water to soak and several hours to cook—a good item to put into a cast-iron pot and simmer over a fire.

Pasta comes in many varieties and stores well. Keep jarred or canned sauces, and you can combine them for an easy meal, although they require a fair amount of water to cook in.

Textured Vegetable Protein (TVP) is a dried soy product that can be purchased in health-food stores. It comes in chunks or flakes and is available in meat flavors or plain, which takes on the flavor of whatever you are cooking with it. TVP can be rehydrated with a little water and used in a variety of ways.

Powdered egg substitutes can be used in baking and can be purchased in regular and health-food stores.

Nonfat powdered milk can be made up and drunk in a pinch, but it is better for cooking. It's not the same as fresh milk, of course, but it stores well.

Canned fruits and vegetables will add greatly to the variety of your emergency pantry for both health reasons and added interest.

TIP
PURCHASE CANNED GOODS IN SIZES TO FIT YOUR FAMILY'S NEEDS.
THROW AWAY RUSTY CANS.

When you want fresh vegetables and nothing is available, store seeds to sprout. These come in many varieties such as radish, mung beans, alfalfa, wheat grass, and broccoli, and are very nutritious. Quite often, you can purchase a sprouting device at a grocery store.

If your budget allows, stock up on spirulina or protein powder, popcorn, dried-soup mixes, canned meats and fish, canned nuts and peanut butter, canned or powdered cheese, dried yeast, honey or sugar, boxed liquid milk substitutes (soy or Rice Dream if you don't drink milk), buttermilk powder, jams and jellies, coffee (see also dandelion coffee, page 64), your favorite teas, powdered drink mixes, and dessert mixes.

How Much Food Will You Need?

Monitor your family's food consumption for a week and multiply it by four for a month's supply. Keep in mind that you can eat *much* less in an emergency situation, but you want to keep enough food on hand to keep everyone fairly happy, especially teenagers. You will not choose the same foods you are used to, because of the shelf-life requirements, but keeping your family's diet close to normal helps keep up spirits.

Food requirements for babies, elders, or folks with unique eating needs will require some additional organization and preparation, according to your particular needs.

STORING AND PRESERVING FOOD

If you grow your own food, you have an advantage. In the "not-so-olden times," it was standard practice to have gardens and preserve the harvest. We have become dependent on the trucking system, our local food stores and our freezers. If there's a major disaster, there may be no trucking system, and the food may not be delivered. Keep in mind that food stores stock approximately three days worth of food. We witness how quickly stores run out of the staples every time a major storm approaches and everyone stocks up on bread and milk!

If your power fails when it is freezing outdoors, put coolers outside to store butter, cheese and other perishable foods as long as the temperature stays below 32°F. If the weather is warm or for folks in warm climates, sticking to canned and dried foods is best.

If you grow your own or purchase local fresh foods, we suggest that you can them. Ideally, you'll need to purchase a pressurized canner, tongs and enough jars and lids for your purposes. Follow the directions for the particular food you are canning. It is very important to get a good seal, so be sure to observe the top of the jar when opening *any* canned food item. If there is any mold, it is best to throw the food away. Canned food should be used and rotated yearly. The benefit of canned food is that it doesn't require cooking, water or any special preparation. You can also freeze your harvest, but much of it could be lost if the electricity is out more than three days.

It is important to follow strict hygienic procedures to avoid contamination. If you do not have a cookbook with instructions for safe canning, you can get them through the US Department of Agriculture,[1] and print them out ahead of time. Keep them with your canner.

---

1. http://tinyurl.com/USDAFoodPreservation

You may consider purchasing a dehydrator to dry food in advance, or it can be done in the oven on warm, with the door open slightly. Dried food can be stored in zip-lock bags or jars. To extend the shelf life of dehydrated food, keep it in the freezer until needed. To rehydrate, just add water or eat it dry.

TIP:
MOST FOOD-BORNE CASES OF BOTULISM COME FROM HOME-CANNED FOODS WITH LOW-ACID CONTENT SUCH AS ASPARAGUS, GREEN BEANS, BEETS AND CORN.

If you are in the country or even suburbia, another traditional way to store fruits and vegetables is in a root cellar. These can be made in a variety of ways with the four main requirements being: cool temperatures, a humidity level above 80%, adequate ventilation, and complete darkness. Obviously, root cellars take advance preparation and may not be feasible for many folks without basements, or places to build one.

STORAGE TIPS FROM FEMA

- Keep food in the driest and coolest spot in the house—a dark area if possible. Keep food covered at all times.

- Open food boxes or cans carefully so that you can close them tightly after each use.

- Wrap cookies and crackers in plastic bags, and keep them in tight containers.

- Empty opened packages of sugar, dried fruits and nuts into screw-top jars or air-tight cans to protect them from pests.

EVACUATED FROM HOME

When you have to get out of town *now*, you may not have much time to begin making up menus for your trip, which is why we have stressed that you should start now to build your portable *Stash*. This should be easily accessible on the way to your vehicle, protected from heat, dampness and wild creatures.

The Portable Food Stash

For your portable *Stash*, choose food items that are light weight, compact, and with long shelf-life. Create as great a variety as you can, within the constraints of your budget and storage method. In case you have to load everything yourself, make sure that you can lift each container. You can take your portable *Stash* with you when you go camping, but remember to replace it when you return.

Stash List:
See page 148.

FINDING FOOD OUTSIDE

If you have a choice, avoid eating things from the sides of roads that may contain exhaust from autos. The leaves of the often despised dandelion are an excellent, nutritious food source (see page 64). If you have been applying toxic chemicals to your lawn, we suggest you soak any yard greens in apple-cider vinegar for about 10 minutes before you eat them, which *may* reduce some of the pesticides, but no guarantees. Better yet, stop using the chemicals and cultivate your lawn as a food source filled with dandelions and clover. When it's cut short, it looks like grass; when you need it, let it grow!

A potentially life-saving trend that is catching on is the edible landscape, where the yard is a landscaped food source. How convenient this would be in a neighborhood during an extended crisis, or even without one!

Hunt and gather! Are there acorns about? Walnuts? Blackberries, huckleberries, raspberries? Apples? Grapes? Know the natural cycles in your area and watch what drops from trees. It may be food, not just something to sweep up. Acorns from White Oak trees (pointy leaves) can be ground up for flour. Nuts can be shelled, stored and eaten. Fruits can be eaten or dried in the sun—preferably with a screen on top to keep the critters away. Some fruits dry more quickly than others, so you'll have to watch. What grows in your area that could be edible?

"Most" plant life is edible. Purchase a local plant identification book for your area so you can learn about the edible plants, and keep it in your *Stash*.

Caution: it is believed by some that you can eat a tiny pinch of a plant, then wait for 12 to 24 hours. If there are no ill effects, you can eat some more. We have also done this, but remember—a few plants are *deadly* in very small quantities, such as water hemlock, poison hemlock and castor bean and oftentimes they look like other plants. So use extreme caution and be certain you know what the plant is before eating it. Eat no mushrooms unless you know what you're doing, and stay away from most red berries in the wild, unless you are familiar with the plant.

If you are absolutely desperate, starving, and you've stored nothing, remember that almost everything that walks, crawls, flies or swims is edible.[1] This may sound completely gross, but consider *entomophagy*—the eating of arthropods— insects, spiders and the like. According to the Entomological Society of America, arthropods generally contain more protein and less fat than traditional meats. Plus, they are 20 times more efficient in food conver-

---

1. http://tinyurl.com/InsectNutrition

sion than traditional meats, *i.e.*, they produce much more nutrition per unit of "feed" than beef, pork, lamb or chicken, and they sustain themselves.

While we were traveling in Thailand, we had the "opportunity" to eat some insect foods. To our big surprise, the fried grubs were actually quite tasty, like a salty snack. We do not recommend giant water bugs pulled from polluted water, however. But when your back is against the wall, all options should be considered. You can find many recipes online for crickets, grasshoppers and the like, including a list of 1462 species of edible insects.[1] If you put enough garlic on something and fry it, almost anything can taste good.

Remember hunger is a greater threat to you psychologically than physically. Depending on your circumstances, such as the temperature and your physical condition, you can go over a month without food. Hunger pains will disappear after about three days. If you have to be walking, building shelters, *etc.*, you'll need fuel for your body. If you are at home lounging about, waiting for life to return to normal, your body will need less food.

1. http://www.insectsarefood.com

10

A Few Useful Plants

EVERYTHING YOU NEED TO KNOW, YOU LEARNED FROM NOAH'S ARK...
LOOK FOR GREEN PLANTS.

Here are a few plants that grow *almost* everywhere—even in our lawns. They can easily help with some health issues when other alternatives are not available. A few more edible and medicinal plants to look for are: common chickweed, grapes, chokecherry, dill, birch, cattails, and dock. There are hundreds more, which is why we emphasize the importance of purchasing a plant book for *your* area that covers what is edible and medicinal.

Dandelion

You will find this plant presenting its beautiful yellow flowers in the spring in many parts of the country. For the most part it is a very maligned plant that we destroy by pouring poisons on our lawns. In so doing, we're losing a vital source of nutrition. It contains Vitamins A (higher than carrots), B, C, and D and helps keep your liver and gall blader strong, which is your body's filtering system.

The leaves and stems are less bitter when picked before the flowers appear in the early spring. They can be added to any salad to give it a slightly bitter taste or added to a sautéed greens mixture. They are loaded with minerals.

The root can also be used as a coffee substitute. Dig up the root (preferably in early spring or late fall when the plant is dormant), wash it and simmer for 20 to 30 minutes. You can use the root fresh or you can dry it by placing on an airy screen until dry.

Mullein

This plant grows along the sides of roads, in fields and maybe, if you're lucky, in your back yard. It has large (up to 12" in length), soft fuzzy leaves that grow smaller towards the top of the plant. It can grow to 7' tall, but first-year plants hug the ground.

Mullein has small yellow flowers that bloom at the top of the stalk. The flowers, leaves and root can be used for medicinal purposes, such as breaking up mucous. However, do not take more than 1/3 of the leaves from any one plant. The leaves can be used fresh or dried and will remain fuzzy even when dried. A tea made from mullein leaves is very good for hoarseness, to loosen tight coughs, bronchitis, asthma and whooping cough. *Caution:* Do not eat mullein seeds, as they are toxic.

Peppermint

Peppermint has square stems, and its leaves are opposite, simple and toothed. Most are invasive perennials that send up new shoots from their spreading roots. They like to be near water, and are fragrant. Peppermint relieves coughs and congestion, eases indigestion and gas, calms stomach muscles, helps digest fat, and accelerates food digestion. It is antibacterial, antiviral, calming and numbing, and it eases aches. Its menthol is antibacterial and antiparasitic, thins mucus, and breaks up phlegm. Enteric-coated (time-delayed) peppermint-oil capsules relieve irritable bowel symptoms like gas, diarrhea, bloating and pain. Menthol is common in decongestants and chest rubs to relieve chest aches experienced during colds and the flu.

It often grows wild, and you'll know it by its distinct taste and smell, but you can also cultivate spearmint or peppermint. You can also purchase it in dried form or in tea bags from a health-food store. Rubbing your fingers over the leaves will confirm it is mint.

Plantain or Snakeweed

This plant grows along roads, in fields, in poor soil, and unfortunately for some, in lawns. The ribwort plantain is tall and slender with rather narrow, ribbed leaves that can be 4" to10" long. The flower stalks are even longer, with seeds at the end. The broad-leaved plantain has broader leaves that form in a rosette around the base of the plant. The seed stalks of this form resemble miniature cattails. Plantain is so plentiful that the Native Americans called it "White Man's footprint," as it seemed to follow white men wherever they went. It can reduce the pain of insect bites, help heal wounds, and stop bleeding.

You can gather fresh leaves as needed, or if you want to be prepared, dry them on screens in the shade. The leaves can be made into a tea (steep in boiling or warm water for 15 minutes) to be used as a diuretic.

Yarrow

You can find yarrow in most parts of North America—even in dry climates—in fields, sunny woodlands, along roadsides and in marginal areas. It grows from 1' to 3' in height and is recognized by its disk-shaped clusters of tiny white, daisy-like flowers. It is sparsely covered with leaves that are about 2" long and 1/2" wide. You may find yarrow blooming in orange, yellow and red colors, but the white is traditionally used to treat colds and congestion, stop bleeding, and to cleanse the blood.

Red Clover

This herb is found in most places in the US in fields and gardens. It has a red blossom and grows about 12" tall. The dried flower heads are used. It makes a very tasty tea. Since it is an expectorant, it is good for coughs and bronchitis. It also helps with skin issues by cleansing the blood and cells.

Stinging Nettle

Nettle leaf is another common, but valuable herb. When it first comes up in the spring its stingers are too soft to hurt you. Later in the summer, you can get an itchy, burny rash if you accidently brush it. It is very nutritious with loads of minerals, making it a good spring tonic, which can cleanse the body of metabolic wastes. Its iron content means it is a good blood builder and its Vitamin C helps with

iron absorption. It is also a diuretic, which increases the secretion and flow of urine in case of bladder or kidney issues. Consider this a food in the early spring.

11

Health

EVERYTHING YOU NEED TO KNOW, YOU LEARNED FROM NOAH'S ARK...
STAY FIT. WHEN YOU'RE OLD, SOMEONE MAY ASK YOU
TO DO SOMETHING REALLY BIG.

Your ability to survive any emergency is enhanced by good health. It is helpful to be able to walk and run, and to see, hear and think clearly. We have outlined four major types of emergency situations you may find yourself in, and health concerns in each case differ somewhat.

If you are caught away from home without a vehicle, then your *Pocket Set*, wits, common sense and knowledge are your best tools for health. If you are stuck in your vehicle, you also have your *Go Pack*, in which you will have a small first-aid kit and your personalized Natural Remedy Kit, both discussed below. Useful knowledge to keep with you would include basic first-aid techniques.

Whether you are stuck at home without utilities or evacuated, you will have access to the portable portion of your *Stash*. In it you should have stored the home remedies that apply to you and your family's needs. You can choose these items either from your over-the counter products that you normally use or refer to "Symptoms & Remedies" (side box) for natural solutions.

Pocket Set:
See page 15.

Go Pack:
See page 145.

Natural Remedy Kit:
See page 70.

Stash:
See page 148.

Symptoms & Remedies:
See page 78.

FIRST-AID KITS

We suggest you purchase two first-aid kits—an extensive one that includes tourniquets, snake-bite kits, *etc.*, for your *Stash*, and a smaller one for your *Go Pack*—and know how to use them. Check the list of first-aid kit add-ins for items that might need to be added to your kit.

It is important to know the dangerous critters in your area and how to treat bites from them. This is another opportunity to keep that subtle observance in the forefront when working in a garden or walking in the woods because knowledge and awareness transforms fear. Look before sitting on rocks or reaching into dark spaces. Walk heavily to announce to any wild creatures in the neighborhood that you are approaching.

EMERGENCY PERSONAL HYGIENE

Go Pack:
See page 145.

Stash List:
See page 148.

You can purchase portable camping toilets starting at $30 and up, depending on capabilities. Some are bulky to carry, but pleasant to use. As we mentioned for your safe-haven room, large plastic buckets with tight-fitting lids make passable commodes and can carry supplies within them. Make sure you have plastic bags with you to make cleaning easier. Camping toilet seats with lids sell online for around $17.00.[1] You can purchase the buckets at home-improvement stores or you can ask your local restaurant if they are throwing any out. You can keep regular toilet paper rolls in the *Stash*, but to save space in your *Go Pack*, you may want to purchase the more expensive, compact rolls you can get at a camping store.

A natural alternative to toilet paper used by pioneers in the summer in many regions is the *buttonweed* plant, with big, soft leaves like elephant ears, however be sure to know what you are using. We know someone who used poison ivy by mistake. It was a nasty event, to say the least.

If your toilets aren't working, or you happen to be in the woods waiting something out, you can always squat outside. Remember to bury your solids at least 6" below the ground with your small folding shovel from your *Go Pack*.

*Buttonweed:
emergency toilet paper*

Don't forget the feminine products that may be needed each month and keep a few extra sanitary pads for major wounds.

EMERGENCY MEDICAL ISSUES

Special Medical
Needs List:
See page 144.

It would help if at least one person in your group takes first-aid classes, CPR, *etc.* Your local Red Cross office should have classes in your area. It's also helpful to learn the difference between life-threatening and non-life-threatening conditions in determining your course of action, decreasing the likelihood of panic and increasing the survivability of an injured person.

---

1. http://tinyurl.com/BarreToiletSeat

It would also be helpful for you to fill in the special medical needs of the primary people in your group, so that if you are suddenly relocated, you can quickly become re-established with your special medical and dental care needs.

TIP

IF YOUR INSURANCE REQUIRES THAT
YOU USE ONLY SOME FACILITIES AND NOT OTHERS,
MAKE SURE THAT THIS INFORMATION IS ON YOUR SPECIAL
MEDICAL NEEDS LIST FOR EMERGENCY RESPONDERS.

If ambulances are disabled or overloaded, you'll need to transport any injured person yourself—properly and safely. Know the location of the nearest emergency facilities. If there is a general emergency in your community, the hospitals will be focused on more critical needs, so patience will be a virtue.

Medical care is a luxury that we take for granted and that we hope will continue. But, we know of an instance when a nearby drugstore's computer system went down, so no meds could be filled that day. There were many disgruntled people. Those who were refilling an on-going prescription experienced a delay of a day or two. Those who were sick and in need of medicine were majorly inconvenienced. Do not assume that computerized systems will operate during crises, so refill you prescriptions before you completely run out.

If you require particular medications, eyeglasses, contact lenses or prosthetics, secure extras in advance and have them in both your *Go Pack* and *Stash* if you can. With medications, getting extras may not be possible, but check with your doctor. When a new prescription for eyeglasses is filled, put the older pair in your *Go Pack* or car in case of emergencies. They'll be a good backup.

In addition to vitamins or medications that you or your children normally take, store enough Vitamins C, A, E, B's, Calcium and Zinc to keep your immune system strong, and fight off diseases. On page 71 we recommend other things you can do to build and strengthen your immune system.

Complex and acute medical situations are beyond the scope of this book. In those cases you must seek medical attention, to the extent that it is available.

In "Symptoms and Remedies" (page 78) you will find an alphabetical section of common conditions that might afflict you during emergencies and simple remedies for them that do not require access to a potentially overloaded or non-functioning medical establishment.

NATURAL REMEDIES

We recommend that you stock a few homeopathic remedies (explained below) and herbal products that will take up a relatively small amount of space in your

Go Pack (page 145) or *Stash*. For instance, a few small vials of homeopathic remedies or a bottle of herbal extract can be held in your closed fist.

Always check with your own health practitioner when taking a new supplement. Our recommendations are for when doctors and the medical emergency systems are not readily available.

Homeopathic Medicine

Homeopathic medicine was founded by Dr. Samuel Hahnemann in the 19th century and was one of the main medical practices at the turn of the 20th century in America. It is based on the belief that substances, which in large doses could create a particular set of symptoms, could also in very minute doses relieve those same symptoms. There are hundreds of these products, and their effectiveness depends upon *how closely you can match your symptoms* to those identified with the remedy. It is important to note that the medically active substances in these remedies occur in such infinitesimally small amounts that they are non-toxic, with no adverse side-effects. And they do work. Thus, in the Symptoms & Remedies chapter (page 78) we have suggested some basic remedies that can be counted on for certain conditions most of the time.

Herbal Extracts

Herbal extracts come in small bottles that can also be purchased at your local-health-food store and sometimes your pharmacy. The herbs are preserved with alcohol to provide more shelf life. For those with alcohol intolerance or for children, you can also purchase them preserved in glycerine. These extracts can be taken with water, which neutralizes the taste.

THE NATURAL REMEDY KIT

On page 151 is our suggested short list of what to procure to outfit a very compact, but useful *Natural Remedy Kit* that will often allow you to help others around you feel better. This kit is intended to be carried in your *Go Pack* (page 145). You may want to provision a more extensive remedy kit for inclusion in your *Stash* (page 148) along with your over-the-counter products.

Symptoms and Remedies, page 78, includes many applications of herbal and homeopathic items, some of which are not in the Natural Remedy Kit. We suggest that you add any such additional items that fit your personal needs.

TIP
THE MOST IMPORTANT HEALTH ITEM YOU CAN KEEP WITH YOU IS
A STRONG IMMUNE SYSTEM.
IT IS YOUR FIRST LINE OF DEFENSE AGAINST BACTERIA, VIRUSES, AND ANY
AIRBORNE BIOLOGICAL TOXINS YOU MIGHT ENCOUNTER.

BUILDING AND PROTECTING YOUR IMMUNE SYSTEM

The indiscriminate overuse of antibiotics has encouraged some bacteria to develop survival-of-the-fittest resistance to all antibiotics (see page 121), making our immune systems our front line. It is made up of T-cells, natural killer cells, and organs that distinguish between "good" cells and invaders that trigger it into action (see also page 128). Immune cells need adequate nutrition for peak performance. Plus, as you'll read in "That Uncertainty in the Air" (page 115), the inclusion of GMOs, dyes and chemical preservatives in our food supply have compromised our normal bodily functions.

The typical American diet of processed foods and too much red meat keeps us very acidic, which can take us out of pH balance and into illness. Therefore, maintaining a good, low-fat, low-sugar, chemical-free (no preservatives) diet with plenty of fresh fruits and vegetables and a low amount of red meat will keep your body more pH-balanced and healthy.

Here are several simple practices you can follow that will help maintain the vitality of your immune system and keep you healthy:

- Exercise regularly and moderately—like a daily 30-minute walk—to increase your level of leukocytes, which fight infection. Being too sedentary reduces your sleep quality, leads to obesity and generally increases your risk of illness.

- Control your weight to reduce your likelihood of developing diabetes, cancer, or heart disease and avoiding joint problems. A high number of fat cells releases inflammatory body chemicals, which leads to chronic inflammation, which damages healthy tissue.

- Avoid foods that are high in white sugar, which suppresses your immune system cells that attack bacteria. Even drinking a couple of 12-ounce sodas significantly reduces for several hours your white blood cells' ability to overpower and destroy bacteria.

- Be careful of labels that use the word "natural," as it is not organic.

- Eat whole grains of all kinds unless you are gluten-intolerant, then you'll have to test which ones work for you, if any.

- Eat smaller fish that contain less mercury, and small amounts of chicken, pork and occasionally red meat. As a general rule, your meat portion should be no larger than a deck of playing cards.

- Use antibiotics only when truly necessary.

- Wash your hands with regular soap. Even doctors are now steering people away from antibacterial soaps.

- Reduce or avoid chronic stress, which makes you more vulnerable to illness by exposing your body to a steady flow of cortisol and adrenaline—stress hormones that suppress your immune system.

- Get plenty of sleep. Most of us need about 7 to 9 hours per night. Most people don't realize that they are sleep deprived.

- Maintain strong *face-to-face* relationships with people. Loneliness can reduce the effectiveness of your immune system.

FOOD

There is a real debate about whether our health is better if we eat organic food. Some studies find no health benefits from organic food *vs.* inorganic food. But *absence of evidence is not evidence of absence.* The benefits of organic food are long-term and subtle, thus impossible to see in short studies. When you eat organically, you avoid the long-term risks from pesticides and herbicides.

Stressing out because you cannot afford organic food will not enhance your health, nor will buying organic and then stressing out over finances. Before the 1960s, all food was organic. It wasn't special in any sense, it was just the way food was grown for thousands of years, and maybe it will be again.

Common sense suggest that we eat as many whole, unprocessed foods, which eliminates preservatives and chemical additives that are so prevalent in packaged food today. Ultimately, it's all a personal choice.

The following supplements and/or food products build up your immune system. We suggest that you choose several that work with your life-style. All the supplements listed should be available at your local health-food store.[1]

Blueberries

Blueberries contain anti-oxidant and anti-inflammatory phytonutrients called polyphenols, which can help lessen chronic conditions. They provide

---

1. We are not addressing vegetarians or vegans, as we feel you are well-versed in your food requirements.

almost 25% of a person's daily requirement of Vitamin C, which can help build our immune systems.

Carrots

Carrots provide Vitamins A, B, C, D, E, G and K. They are often recommended for children and adults to correct gastric disturbances and help improve resistance to infections, but especially with the eyes, throat, sinuses and the respiratory system. Intestinal and liver complaints often arise from too much processed foods and too much alcohol. The beta carotene in carrots supports your liver and also helps the thymus boost immunity, and increases T-cells and natural killer cells. Carrots are best eaten raw and chewed well.

Garlic

Garlic, often called the most important plant on the planet, is vital for strengthening our bodies and fighting off disease by building our immune system, in addition to flavoring our food. It is naturally antibacterial and antiviral. It is an antioxidant, which prevents the formation of harmful free radicals in the body. It is rich in selenium, promotes the building of energy in the body, and helps retain vital B vitamins. Each clove contains vitamins B1, B2, B3, C and other minerals, plus all eight essential amino acids and the highest sulphur content in any vegetable. It also helps expel parasites. More than any other food, garlic fulfills Hippocrates's requirement for a perfect food, that it should be our medicine—and that our medicine should be our food.

Garlic is an excellent addition to food when you have a cold, flu or just feel like you're getting sick. You can eat it raw (it's actually not bad, eaten on apple slices) or you can purchase it in "odorless" extracts or capsules. It's good to have around in whatever form you desire. To dispel garlic and onion breath, eat some parsley or drink peppermint tea.

Maitake mushrooms

These mushrooms contain natural substances known as polysaccharides, which are thought to help fight disease. One of these polysaccharides is believed to be particularly potent in its ability to stimulate the immune system. These can be found in health-food stores and can be added to your recipes. They can be dried to increase shelf life.

Onion

The powerful sulfur compound of onions that brings tears to your eyes is also believed to be responsible for healing skin infections and fighting colds, sore throats, high blood pressure, bronchitis and cancer. Onions are rich in allicin, which helps lower cholesterol levels. They also contain a beneficial antioxidant and anti-inflammatory bioflavonoid that contributes to cardiovascular health. It is believed that eating onions regularly can help purify the blood, lower high blood pressure, and normalize elevated blood sugar. Onions also stimulate the gastric secretions of the stomach and therefore improve digestion, while eliminating gas. Onions can also be a good diuretic, reducing bloating and swelling of the extremities. Some say that just cutting an onion in half and leaving it in your room can help by soaking up bacteria floating in the air. Dried onions store well long-term.

Pumpkin Seeds

These seeds are high in vitamins A and E, plus zinc and Omega-3 fatty acids, which are all immune-boosting nutrients. You may find them at your grocery or health-food stores. They can be added to salads, eaten raw or roasted with a little salt. Roasted seeds will last longer.

Seaweed

Seaweed may be an acquired taste for most of us, but it can be used in soups, salads and side dishes and as a sushi wrapper. There are many varieties to choose from, especially if you are lucky enough to have an Asian market nearby. Each variety has a unique taste and texture, but all of them are valuable sources of nutrients. Most seaweeds are high in essential amino acids, contain vitamins A and C, and are rich in potassium, iron, calcium, iodine and magnesium, all of which help keep your immune system strong. They are also one of the few vegetable sources of vitamin B-12, important for vegetarians.

A benefit from eating seaweed is that it can be used as a salt substitute, which is important, because too much salt in the diet increases your risk of high blood pressure, heart attacks and strokes.

TIP
KEEP RAW SEEDS REFRIGERATED.

HERBAL EXTRACTS OR CAPSULES

Astragalus

TIP
ASTRAGALUS IS NOT RECOMMENDED IF YOU TAKE IMMUNOSUPPRESSANTS.

This herb is classified as one of the "superior ones" in ancient Chinese medicine, and, taken as a preventative, it has been known in clinical trials to fight colds and upper respiratory infections. Astragalus also supports immune function by stimulating the production of natural killer cells and T-cells. It is gentle enough to take daily, and you can find it in children's versions.

Co-enzyme Q10 (CoQ10)

CoQ10 is a vitamin-like substance that is found in your body's cells. Our bodies produce it, but as we age, its production slows. A deficiency of CoQ10 depresses your immune system. You can receive some from food — beef, oily seafood, peanuts, and soy oil, *e.g.*, but not much. CoQ10 has also been known to increase energy and assist in wound healing.

Echinacea

Echinacea was used widely by Native Americans and Europeans for centuries. It was introduced to American medical practice in 1887 and continued to be a top cold and flu remedy until antibiotics became popular. It is now included in so many products that it is on the edge of being overused.

Research shows that it stimulates the production of white blood cells that fight infection. Take it when you feel you may be getting a cold, flu or sore throat. It is great to boost your immune system, but do not use it long-term.

Goldenseal

Goldenseal is a most vital plant that is antibacterial and antiviral. It is being overly wild crafted (dug up in the woods) and is endangered. As antibiotics become less effective due to overuse, more virulent strains of pathogens develop, and the value of this plant will continue to increase. You can purchase the powder at health-food stores. It is *expensive*, but you only need a very small amount—as little as 1 oz. will last a long time. It excellent for inflamed mucous membranes.

Grape seed

Grape seeds contain potent antioxidants, which are substances that neutralize and eliminate harmful free radicals that damage cells and DNA and may contribute to aging and illnesses like heart disease and cancer. Free radicals are waste products that the body produces in response to environmental toxins or while converting food to energy. Vitamin E and flavonoids are important antioxidants in grape seeds. Grape seeds have a protective effect on blood vessels, which can help prevent high blood pressure.

SUPPLEMENTS

Melatonin

When the pineal gland detects darkness, it releases melatonin, which sweeps up disease-causing free radicals in your body while we sleep. Some scientists believe that RF emanations from cell-phone towers and wireless devices confuse the pineal gland into thinking it is always daytime,[1] so melatonin is not being produced as it once was. You may think about supplementing at night. Melatonin production naturally declines with age as well.

Selenium

Selenium is an antioxidant that helps prevent free-radical damage and supports the immune function. It also works with Vitamin E in protecting against cellular damage.

Spirulina

This powder can be purchased at health-food stores and is believed to enhance mineral absorption and act as an antioxidant. We often add it to smoothies, or just put a heaping teaspoon into a glass of water and drink.

Vitamin C

In addition to its healing capabilities for flus, colds, *etc.*, Vitamin C enhances antibody responses and assists the immune system by stimulating white-blood-cell activities to combat stress.

Vitamin E

Vitamin E helps remove toxic substances from the blood system and may increase the resistance to infection. It is beneficial to take this vitamin daily.

NATURAL DEFENSES AGAINST UNNATURAL THREATS

In the 1st edition of this book, we were concerned with the possibility of finding anthrax in the mail, or nerve gases in subways. Since we never know what may happen and since our bodies are under toxic attack every day just by living in our chemical-laden, modern environment, we have included the following list of foods that can help fight toxic attacks of any kind. These foods can be included in your diet on a regular basis:

Carrots and Cabbage

When rats were given harmful chemicals in their diets, their symptoms of loss of weight, extensive diarrhea and poor appearance were completely reversed when given carrot and cabbage powders.

---

1. http://tinyurl.com/ResonanceRFdocumentary 90-minute video

Rye and Whole-Grain Wheat

Factory workers in Russia who are exposed to toxic chemicals are urged to eat rye and whole-wheat breads (as well as carrots) in their diets. Doctors and nutritionists there believe these foods have a neutralizing and eliminating effect on harmful chemicals.

Garlic

Russian electrobiologist Professor Gurwitch discovered that garlic emits a peculiar type of ultra-violet mitogenetic radiation,[1] now referred to as Gurwitch rays, which stimulates cell growth and activity and has a rejuvenating effect on all body functions. (See page 73.)

Ginger and Ginseng

Both medicinal roots emit a strong mitogenetic radiation. Ginger can be found in root form at your grocery. Pour boiling water over about 4 - 6 slices (1/4" thick) in a cup and let steep for 5 - 10 minutes. You can drink this every day if you wish. You can also just grate fresh ginger over your food. Ginseng can be purchased in capsule form and taken daily when you feel under attack by too many toxins

YOUR FRIEND: THE PLACEBO

A placebo (pluh-see-bow) looks like a regular treatment or medicine, but is not. Your belief in it as an effective medicine helps change your condition. According to the American Cancer Society,[2] placebos affect about 33% of patients who were given no medicine but were just told that they were. This is just quantum mechanics (see page 113). The medical industry has long ignored them, but a free chance at a 1-in-3 effect is worth taking. A .333 batting average is very respectable.

The placebo effect in health studies has really been advising us for years that if we believe that what we are taking or being given is healing us, we heal.

---

1. http://tinyurl.com/MitogeneticRadiation
2. http://tinyurl.com/ACSplacebo

12

Symptoms and Remedies

EVERYTHING YOU NEED TO KNOW, YOU LEARNED FROM NOAH'S ARK...
WHEN YOU SEE A PROBLEM, FIND A SOLUTION.

Here you will find simple, inexpensive, natural ways to relieve common ailments and distressful conditions that you or your family might encounter while stuck at home or evacuated without easy access to medical assistance or pharmacies. When you encounter complex or acute medical situations, you must seek medical attention, to the extent that it is available.

The homeopathic (defined on page 70) remedies listed here can be purchased at most health-food stores. They will be listed with the symptom that you are trying to relieve. They cost about $6.00 to $8.00 each and consist of tiny pellets that you place under your tongue and allow to dissolve. The symptoms are listed in detail because you are trying to closely match them.

It is important not to drink or eat anything (don't even brush your teeth) for approximately 15 minutes before or after taking these to make them more effective. And do not touch the pellets with your hands—just use the cap to drop them in your mouth. Your skin chemistry can change the chemistry of the medicine.

Homeopathics are sold in potencies of 3C, 6C, 12C or 30C. The lower potencies may need to be used more frequently. If the condition does not improve after one or two doses, try something else. *Also, please note child dosages should be 3C or 6C.*

Allergies: Pollen And Hay Fever

Food: Honey

Honey is a natural antibiotic and will not spoil.[1] It is widely useful as a food, an antiseptic and an accelerator for healing wounds. If you suffer from pollen allergies, it may help you to find a source of local honey and eat a tablespoon or more of it every day. When your body produces histamines in an

---

1. *Caution:* because honey can contain spores of *Clostridium botulinum* (botulism), children less than a year old should *not* be given honey. Note: older honey will crystallize, but can be slightly heated to remove the crystals.

allergic reaction, it is signalling you that it thinks it has encountered an invasion of something foreign, which must be counter-attacked. The key observation is that you can retrain your body to regard local pollens as *food* rather than as invaders. If you do this, your body will not react the same way any more. You retrain your body's defense system by regularly eating *local* honey. Local honey is key, because it is made of the local plants that are bothering you.

Homeopathic Remedy: BioAllers

This can be purchased at your local health-food store in liquid form. It is very effective for hay fever. Dosage: Take 15 drops under your tongue every 3 - 4 hours during hay-fever season.

Household Solution: Salt

Neti Pots have been used in India for centuries and look like tiny tea pots and are available in health-food stores. Irrigate your sinuses by tilting your head to one side (then the other) over a sink and pouring the saltwater solution through one side of your nose then through the opposite. This will clear out pollen and soothe nasal passages. Thoroughly dissolve a slightly heaping 1/4 tsp. of salt into a Neti Pot full of lukewarm water. Use sea, Kosher, or pickling salt. It should not be iodized or contain any caking agents. Use boiled tap water, filtered bottled or distilled water. If you need to boil it, make sure it cools down to lukewarm.

Wild Plant: Stinging Nettle (Also see page 66.)

This plant contains compounds that inhibit histamines, which can help with itchy eyes, runny nose and congested sinuses. You can also purchase it at health-food stores in capsule form.

Appendicitis

Symptoms may include: severe, dull, constant pain usually on right side, rigidity in lower right side, a fever of 101° or higher, loss of appetite, indigestion, nausea, vomiting. Most appendices are located in the lower right area of the abdomen, but don't depend on pain on the right side to definitely indicate appendicitis. Seek medical care, if available.

Asthma

If someone in your family suffers from asthma, make sure you have extra supplies of medication in the person's *Go Pack* and *Stash*.

If you are without medical care, making a tea from mullein leaves and straining it afterwards to remove fine hairs can help reduce the inflammation.

Bee Stings, Insect Bites

First remove the bee stinger with a sterile tweezer, taking care not to squeeze further venom into the skin. Wasps leave no stingers.

Wild Plant: Plantain or Snakeweed

The *crushed* leaves can be applied directly to the skin to relieve the pain of bee stings and insect bites. Cover with gauze or a clean cloth if needed. The plant has tremendous drawing power as a poultice to pull poisons out.

Herbal extract: Echinacea

Use this antibacterial extract externally for cleansing and treating insect stings, bites and snake bites. This can be diluted slightly with water.

Homeopathic remedy: Apis Mellifica 30C

Recommended for insect bites, hives, and sunburn. It is to be used for irritated skin that is bright pink, burning, and itching; and where irritation is improved by cold applications. *Dosage:* Five pellets every 15 min. up to 6 doses.

Essential Oil: Neem Oil

This can be purchased at most health-food stores and is excellent for chigger bites, as it smothers the microscopic creature under your skin. It can also be applied to rashes and other insect bites. It can also prevent bites when applied to the skin, but be warned, it has a strong odor.

Essential Oil: Peppermint (See also page 65.)

Living in the south, we would not be without this oil that is used to relieve the sting and itchiness from insect bites, especially chiggers. It also helps heal bites faster.

Household Product: Nail Polish

Nail polish can relieve chigger bites by suffocating the little buggers. This method works, but you may be applying toxins to your skin.

Household Solution: Adolf's Meat Tenderizer

This spice that many people have in their cabinet is very effective on bee stings and insect bites.

Household Solution: Baking Soda

Make a paste with a little water and baking soda and apply to an insect bite or sting.

Household Solution: Vinegar

Dabbing some vinegar onto a bite can relieve itching.

Nature Solution: Mud

Apply moistened mud to an insect or bee sting to relieve the pain and draw out the venom.

Biological Threats

If you suspect an illness to be related to bioterrorism, contact your local health authorities **immediately,** or call the Center for Disease Control (CDC) at 800-CDC-INFO. The information included here on biological threats is courtesy of the CDC.

Anthrax

- **Symptoms from skin contact:** the powder can infect a cut which will turn into a raised rash that will begin to develop into a black scab.
- **Symptoms from Inhalation:** are similar to flu—fever, headaches, chills, vomiting, chest or abdominal pain.
- **Treatment:** Contact your local health authorities. The current drugs available have bad side effects that cause nausea, diarrhea and dizziness. Skin infections can be treated with penicillin or doxycycline. There are antibiotic-resistant strains, so use antibiotics only when you really need them. Cipro is the only FDA-approved antibiotic for Anthrax, but according to military experts, it is likely to be ineffective if the victim already shows any symptoms.

Botulism

Botulism is a rare, but serious paralytic illness. Food-borne botulism comes from eating foods that contain the botulism toxin. Wounds can become infected with *Clostridium botulinum,* and infant botulism is caused by consuming the spores of the botulinum bacteria. All forms can be fatal and should be considered medical emergencies. About 25% of the 110 or so annual cases are food borne, 72% are infant botulism, and the rest are wound botulism.

- **Symptoms:** double vision, blurred vision, drooping eyelids, slurred speech, difficulty swallowing, dry mouth and muscle weakness. Infants with botulism appear lethargic, feed poorly, are constipated and have a weak cry and poor muscle tone. Symptoms from food botulism generally appear 18 to 36 hours after eating contaminated food, but it can be as quick as 6 hours or as long as 10 days.

- **Treatment:** Seek medical care quickly. Physicians may remove food by inducing vomiting or using enemas. Wounds should be treated, usually surgically, to remove the source of the toxin-producing bacteria.

Plague

Pnuemonic plague occurs when *Yersinia pestis* infects the lungs.

- **Symptoms:** first signs of the illness are fever, headache, weakness and a cough that contains bloody or watery sputum. The pneumonia progresses over 2 to 4 days and may cause septic shock. *Early treatment is essential.*
- **Treatment:** Several antibiotics are effective, including streptomycin, tetracycline and cloramphenicol, but there is no plague vaccine.

Ricin

Ricin is a highly toxic poison that can be cheaply and simply produced from castor beans. Although deadly in large quantities, ricin is less dangerous than anthrax, smallpox, or botulism. On April 16, 2013, three envelopes of ricin were intercepted on their way to President Obama, Miss. Sen. Roger Wicker and a judge in Mississippi. In 1978, A Bulgarian journalist was killed in London by being injected with a pellet of ricin from an umbrella.

- **Symptoms:** difficulty breathing, fever, nausea, and coughing, typically within 10 hours, followed by fluid buildup in the lungs and heavy sweating. As the symptoms progress, low blood pressure and respiratory failure can cause death.
- **Treatments:** There is no antidote. Remove the toxin from the body as soon as possible; give intravenous fluid, flush the stomach, and support breathing with ventilation. Seek fresh air immediately, cut off clothing that might be tainted, sealing it in a plastic bag. Wash skin with soap and water and seek medical attention as soon as possible. According to the CDC, do not induce vomiting, but administer a single dose of activated charcoal as soon as possible if the patient has ingested it, vomiting has not begun, and the airway is clear. [1]

Smallpox

- **Symptoms:** The incubation period is 12 to 14 days. Initial symptoms include high fever, fatigue, and head and back aches. After 2 to 3 days of fever, red rashes form. There can be boils on the face, arms,

---

1. http://emergency.cdc.gov/

legs and palms of hands. The person is thirsty, but can't swallow, can have sores in the mouth and throat, and blistered eyelids.

- **What to do:** Contact public health officials if you suspect smallpox.
- **Prevention:** encourage your government representatives to bring back the vaccine, which is the only way to prevent this disease. If the vaccine is administered within 3 to 4 days of exposure, it can lessen the severity or even prevent the disease. Build up your immune system.
- **Treatments:** There is no proven treatment for smallpox. Patients receive supportive therapy—intravenous fluids, medicine to control pain or fever. Native Americans, 90% of whom died of smallpox, used the following herbs to ease pain, circulate blood and decrease blistering:
- Oils: Calendula, St. John's Wort, and Tea Tree oil can topically be applied to the blisters.
- Catnip (*Nepeta cataria, L.*) and Saffron are said to be excellent in treating smallpox, as they act as a stimulant, tonic (invigorating and strengthening), and promote perspiration that releases toxins.
- Goldenseal (*Hydrastis canadensis, L.*) was chewed to relieve mouth sores, and was used as a lotion for treating skin eruptions, which helped prevent pitting of the skin.
- Juniper (*Juniperus communis, L.*) berries were used for fumigating the body to ward off contagion. It was suggested by S. Kneip in *My Water Cure* (1897) that 6 to 10 berries should be chewed throughout the day, which will "burn up as it were, the harmful miasms, exhalations, when these seek to enter through the mouth or nostrils."
- Virginia snakeroot (*Aristolochia serpentaria*) is used to divert the flow of blood outward and therefore is used with disruptive diseases before anything is actually visible. It is also a nerve stimulant and is used in depressed or exhausted conditions during the latter stages of smallpox.
- Yarrow (*Achillea millefolium, L.*) was found to be useful with smallpox as a blood cleanser, increasing perspiration to release waste and helping keep up bodily strength.

Tularemia

Tularemia is a serious infectious disease found in rabbits and similar animals in North America. It is passed to humans through contact with infected animal tissues or by ticks, biting flies, or mosquitoes. *Francisella tularensis* is a potential bioterrorism agent that could be spread by aerosol release. Pneumonia symptoms start 1 to 10 days after exposure.

- **Symptoms:** fever, fatigue, chills, headache, and malaise.
- **Treatment:** Streptomycin and tetracycline. Seek medical care.

Bladder Infections

If you are prone to bladder infections, you may want to have an ample supply of cranberry juice in your *Stash*, to be taken at the first sign of a problem. An alternative is apple-cider vinegar (see below). Keeping your urine acidic is a major part of curing your infection—along with flushing with large amounts of water. Alkalinity in the body is usually healthier than acidity, except in this case. It's about balance. Also take Vitamin C, A and B6. If you do not have access to antibiotics or Chinese herbs, the following can help.

Wild Plant: Plantain

Leaves can be used as a diuretic when made into a tea (steep in boiling or warm water for 15 minutes).

Apple-Cider Vinegar

Drink 2 to 3 tbsp. in 8 oz. of water. It will be sour, but you'll soon adjust.

Homeopathic Remedy: Cantharis 30C

For urinary trouble with a non-stop desire to urinate, burning, cutting pains in lower abdomen, and a sensation that your bladder cannot be emptied. (See also burns, scalds, sunburns, below.) Dosage: 5 pellets every 30 min., up to 10 doses.

Homeopathic Remedy: Nux Vomica 6C

For urinary trouble—frequent urge to urinate with little urine produced, chills, irritability, extremely critical of others, a desire to be left alone. Dosage: 5 pellets every 30 min., for up to 10 doses.

Note: these remedies will "flush" your whole system—meaning your bowels may move as well!

Broken Bones

Broken bones need to be immobilized as best you can in a splint and will need professional medical care. Refer to the first-aid booklet in your *Go Pack*.

Burns, Scalds, Sunburns

It may be helpful to keep a bottle of aloe vera in your *Stash* in case of sunburns. For burns, immerse the wound in cold running water to reduce the pain and cool the burn.

The following are two homeopathic remedies for minor burns and scalds.

- **Symptoms:** the burn may form a blister, has a searing pain, and applying a cold compress soothes the pain.

Homeopathic remedy: Arnica 30C

Dosage: 5 pellets every 15 min., up to 3 doses, followed by:

Homeopathic remedy: Cantharis 30C

Dosage: 5 pellets every 15 min. up to 6 doses; decrease when symptoms improve.

Homeopathic remedy: Apis Mellifica 30C

Recommended for sunburn and burning skin.

- **Symptoms:** irritated skin that is bright pink, burning, and itching; and where irritation is improved by cold applications. Dosage: 5 pellets every 30 min., up to 6 doses.

Herbal Extract: Calendula:

A great herb that is antiseptic and antibacterial. We recommend you buy it in extract form. Dilute it slightly in cool water and apply directly to the skin. *Caution:* Avoid during pregnancy.

Nature Solution: Aloe Vera

Many people have this plant in their kitchen. Cut a small section of leaf and apply the center gel-like portion directly on the burn, or sunburn. The gel is a remarkable healing substance, and encourages skin regeneration.

Food: Honey

This can have spectacular and quick results on burns. Just apply a thin coating as soon as possible.

Burns, Serious

- If the burn is second- or third-degree, or bigger than the palm of a hand, seek medical care immediately, if possible. If that is impossible, spray cold water on the affected area until the heat is reduced, which stops the continued burning of all layers of the skin.
- Then, separate the whites from the yolks of as many eggs as you can gather. Beat them into a froth and spread it onto the affected areas. Continue for at least the first hour to apply layer upon layer of beaten egg whites. Egg white is a natural collagen that aids and

jump-starts the immediate healing process, while protecting the skin at the same time.

Canker Sores or Cold Sores (Herpes simplex virus 1)

Household Solution: Baking Soda

Excellent as a mouthwash when you have canker sores. Mix about 1 tsp. of baking soda in a glass of warm water and frequently rinse.

Do: Eat whole foods, get plenty of sleep, avoid stress. Use an SPF lip balm when outdoors a lot. Eat lysine-rich foods like chicken, sardines, tuna and turkey. Drink astragalus tea throughout the day. Take 1 g. of lysine three times daily as a preventative measure. Take vitamins A and C to boost your immune system. At the first sign of itching, apply lemon balm (*Melissa officianalis*)[1] or Carmex. Keep area covered for several days, and it will almost always retreat.

Don't: Eat arginine-rich foods like chocolate, nuts, seeds, and soy. (Sorry.) Do not kiss anyone (sorry again) or share food when the sores are active. It is a periodic, but recurring, irritation, once acquired.

Household Solution: Table Salt

Mixed with warm water (1 tsp. to 8 oz. of water), salt is an excellent mouthwash for canker sores.

Chemical Threats/ Nerve Agents

Exposure to high doses of nerve agents causes convulsions, rapid loss of consciousness, and suffocating muscular paralysis. There is no realistic treatment. If you see people on the ground with these symptoms, cover your nose and mouth with your *Pocket Set* bandana, preferably uncontaminated and wet, and get out quickly, moving out of the area and upwind. You cannot help the victims, so just grab as many unaffected people as you can on your way out.

Symptoms of minor nerve-agent exposure include excess salivation, runny nose, breathing difficulty, contracted pupils, impaired night vision, pain when focusing on close objects, headaches, fatigue, slurred speech, nausea and hallucinations. If you are suffering from these symptoms, cover your nose and mouth as above, get out of the contaminated area, discard your modesty and drop your clothes and leave them as soon as you get away from the area. Then quickly wash yourself thoroughly in the best way you can.

Immediately seek medical care, if available.

---

1. http://tinyurl.com/EnzymaticColdSoreRelief

Chlorine

- Most of us know the smell of chlorine from swimming pools, so watch for a very sharp odor and watery eyes. Brian nearly died from chlorine-gas inhalation as a teenager, and his lungs were hurt.
- **Symptoms:** mild exposure may cause only coughing and choking. Higher exposure can cause fluid to accumulate in the lungs, therefore breathing will be labored and victims can choke to death.
- **What to do:** Get in an upstairs room, if possible. Stuff any gaps under the doors with towels covered with baking soda that will soak up the chlorine. If you are outside, get in a car. Determine which way the wind is blowing (see page 32) and move upwind at right angles to the wind. Make a face mask out of your bandana or any material you have and wet it. Take a long shower if you can—the water will keep the vapor away.

Sarin

This was the chemical used by Iraq's Saddam Hussein during the Halabja massacre of Kurds in 1988, by Aum Shinrikyo in the Tokyo subways in 1995, and by Syria's President Bashar al-Assad against rebels in 2013.

- **Symptoms:** mild exposure can cause blurry vision and a runny nose. Higher exposure causes nausea, convulsions, vomiting and lung paralysis. A person can die within 2 or 3 minutes after being doused.
- **What to do:** If you see a person up to 50 feet away fall down and other people around that person gagging, leave the scene. It is best to remove all your clothes, as rescue workers have been sickened by contact with victims' clothes. Or wash your clothes, hair and body with *any* water you can find.

Colds, Sinus Problems and Chest Congestion

Symptoms: the common cold comes on gradually—your nose is running, your throat is scratchy, you can have a slight headache from the congestion, and a slight cough can develop as your early symptoms retreat. A cold is *not* usually accompanied by muscle aches, chills and fever, sensitivity to light, appetite loss, or heavy fatigue, although you can feel dull and tired. If you are prone to bronchitis, it can move to your chest, so use caution. Breathing deeply very often can help prevent the congestion lodging deep in the chest.

Essential Oil: Eucalyptus

This oil can be purchased at your health-food store and kept in your *Go Pack* or *Stash*. It is used as an inhalant for colds and sinus problems, which will help keep nasal passages open. It can be rubbed on the skin for chest colds, but dilute slightly with a carrier oil (cooking oil) because it can be strong.

Herb: Elderberry

This can be purchased in bottle form at your pharmacy or health-food store and is very effective in stopping or reducing the length of colds and flu. It inhibits virus replication and has antioxidant properties.

Food: Ginger

Ginger tea is very effective in relieving mucous build-up and painful sinus-itis. For one individual, place 4 to 6 slices (about 1/4" thick) of ginger in a tea cup and add boiling water. Let steep, covered, for about 10 min., and drink. Repeat again every 2-1/2 hours.

Food: Honey

To relieve hoarseness and reduce coughing, you can add honey to tea or even hot water and lemon. You can also use honey as a syrup, with lemon juice, if you have some.

Honey syrup to relieve coughing and to heal: peel some garlic cloves and place them in a clean jar. Cover the garlic with honey. Keep the jar in a sunny window until the garlic is slightly opaque and the honey has a garlic taste. You can dilute this syrup with a little water for children. (Remember honey is not for babies under one year old.)

Food: Onion Syrup

Place a thinly sliced onion in a jar and layer alternately with honey. Allow the mixture to sit overnight. Pour off the syrup the next day—it will keep and remain potent for three days. Take 1 tsp. of syrup every two or three hours. It is very effective for colds, bronchitis and coughs.

Saline Nasal Spray

This can be purchased at most drug or food stores. It is good to keep in your *Go Pack*, especially if you have sinus trouble or often get colds, because it helps loosen head congestion, helps clean nasal passages during pollen season, and helps alleviate nasal dryness in winter or in dry climates.

Herb: Goldenseal

This most-vital plant is antibacterial and anti-viral. It is expensive, but remember you only need a small amount—1 or 2 oz.

Especially good for sinus infections: Into a pan add 1/8 tsp. of Goldenseal powder, 1/8 to 1/4 tsp. non-iodized sea salt and 8 oz. of water. Bring to a boil and let simmer for 10 minutes. Strain through a fine cloth if you can, if not, cool it to room temperature, and the herb will settle to the bottom. You can pour off the clear liquid into a sterilized jar. Either cleanse your nasal passages with a Neti Pot or snuff this mixture into each nostril and hold for 30 seconds or so by holding your head upside down over the sink. Gently blow your nose when finished. One or two doses can be quite effective.

Herbal Extract or Capsule: Echinacea

Echinacea is good for relieving mucous in the nose, sinuses, lungs and digestive tract. We recommend that you take this when you feel you are coming down with an illness. Take a dropperful 2 to 3 times a day at the first sign of illness. The strong taste of the extract is minimized by diluting it in a little water. It also comes in pill form.

Homeopathic remedy: Belladonna 12C - 30C

Take this for colds and illnesses that come on suddenly.

- **Symptoms:** head congestion, mild fever, over sensitivity to noise and light. Dosage: five pellets every hour; decrease with improvement.

Household Solution: Table Salt

Mix 1/8 to 1/4 tsp. in 8 oz. of water to flush your sinuses during a sinus infection (see Goldenseal and Neti Pots, page 88) or to help clear your nasal passages of phlegm during a cold.

Supplement: Zinc

This mineral is very effective when taken at the first sign of illness. It also is an antioxidant that helps rid the body of free radicals. Scientists believe zinc is so effective with colds and sore throats because it attaches to the same nose and throat receptors that the viruses love to occupy, therefore keeping them out. It also enhances wound healing.

Wild Plant: Mullein

Crush the dried leaves (or flowers) and steep them in boiling water until the water is pale yellow. Or place torn pieces of fresh leaf in boiling water until the water is yellow. Drink as a tea to break up respiratory mucous and hoarseness. It is also antiviral. Drink 3 to 4 cups a day while sick. *Caution:* Do not eat mullein seeds, as they are toxic.

Constipation

Nature Solution: Water

First and foremost, make sure you are drinking enough water—8 to 10 glasses a day, even if you are away from home.

Food: Dried Prunes, Whole Grains and Vegetables

Prunes are not only nutritious, but for most people they can also be quite effective in relieving constipation—by only taking 3 a day. Dried prunes can keep quite a while in your *Stash*.

Eating whole grains and fresh vegetables, especially greens can keep you regular due to the fiber.

Wild Plant: Dandelion

Dandelion makes a mild laxative and bitter tonic that is good for the liver. Dig up the root, wash it off, cut it into pieces and steep in boiling or warm water for 15 minutes. If you do not have boiling water, steep it in cold water for 24 hours (if you can wait that long) and drink.

This root taken as above in tea form will stimulate the production of gastric juices, cleanse the blood and detoxify the entire system.

Wild Plant: Plantain

The seeds (or psyllium) have been used in Appalachia for years as a laxative. Soak 2 tsps. of unground seeds in a cup of warm water for *at least* 5 minutes, strain, then drink the liquid. The dose can be repeated up to 3 times a day. Psyllium can be found at health stores. *Caution:* Inhaling psyllium powder can cause asthma, and *unsoaked* seeds can cause gastrointestinal problems.

Cuts and Wounds

First, stop the bleeding with pressure. If it is a major wound, use the tourniquet from your First-aid kit. Seek medical help for large gaping wounds, if it is available. If not, do the best you can to hold the skin together. Skin begins reattaching within hours.

Herbal Extract: Calendula

Since this herb is antiseptic and antibacterial, it is also a good first aid to apply directly to a wound. *Caution:* Avoid during pregnancy.

Food: Honey

Honey can be used to accelerate healing of major wounds, if stitches are not required. It is naturally antibacterial.

Herbal Extract: Echinacea

Echinacea is a good antibacterial cleansing agent for treating wounds and ulcers. Dilute it with a little water and dab on skin.

Household Solution: Sugar

Refined white sugar is known to be effective in rapidly healing deep wounds. Pack the wound with sugar and cover it.

Wild Plant: Plantain or Snakeweed

The *crushed* leaves can be applied directly to the skin to relieve the pain of bee stings and other insect bites and to help heal wounds and stop bleeding. If using dried leaves on wounds or bites, moisten them, then apply to skin. Cover with gauze or a cloth.

Wild Plant: Yarrow

This plant was called soldier's woundwort, as its reputation for stopping bleeding was renowned. You can mash fresh leaves and apply them directly to wounds. You can also dry the herb and apply the dried, powdered herb to cuts, punctures or abrasions.

Diarrhea

Allow your digestive track to release its contents and rest—it is the body's natural mechanism for releasing toxins. Eating a banana will often quickly stop diarrhea. You can cook rice or barley, as if you were cooking pasta in water, and then drink the water. A major concern with diarrhea is dehydration—ingest water as often as possible. If you are not in a position to allow the diarrhea to stop naturally, see below. If you suffer from acute diarrhea that lasts more than 24 hours, or your stool contains blood, or you suffer from chronic diarrhea, seek medical care, if available. The following homeopathic remedies should be in your First-Aid kit and *Go Pack*.

Food: Honey (raw unpasteurized)

Drinking a honey mixture has been known to be very effective in stopping bacterial diarrhea. Put up to 4 heaping tbsps. in a glass of 8 oz. of pure water. Stir it thoroughly and drink as much as you can. *Caution:* those with diabetes should be very careful in ingesting this much honey at one time, and do not give to infants under one year of age.

Homeopathic remedy: Veratrum Album 30C:

Use this in cases of diarrhea associated with crampy abdominal pains. It is very effective. Dosage: 5 pellets 2 to 4 times a day.

Homeopathic remedy: Arsenicum Album 6C

Use with simultaneous diarrhea and vomiting.

- **Symptoms:** chilliness, restlessness, thirst for small frequent sips of water, burning pain in abdomen. Dosage: 5 pellets every hour, up to 10 doses.

Earaches

Food: Garlic and Olive Oil

This combination has been curing ear infections for centuries, and scientific studies have proven that it is still one of the best remedies for ear infections. "The compounds present in garlic oil are absorbed via the eardrum in the inner part of the ear and the nearby tissues which help in healing the infection. Garlic-oil ear drops are known to heal many ear problems like earache, clogged ear, presence of earwax, *etc.*"[1] Place one clove of garlic (preferably organic) into 1/2 cup of pure olive oil and let sit for 1 or 2 days. Then place a few drops of warmed (but not hot) oil in the ears. This can be kept in the refrigerator, otherwise it will only keep for 1 to 2 weeks. It can also be purchased at health-food stores. Caution: do *not* use oil if you suspect a *broken* eardrum.

Flatulence, Gastroenteritis, General Stomach Disorders

Dried Herb or Wild Plant: Peppermint (See also page 65.)

For indigestion, it is well known that peppermint settles the stomach and relieves flatulence and colic, because it is antispasmodic on the smooth muscles of the digestive system. Peppermint is safe to use for infants and young children, but it tends to be a little strong, so dilute accordingly depending on the age of the child.

Dried Herb or Tea Bags: Chamomile

Making a tea of chamomile can sooth indigestion and stomach cramps.

Food: Ginger

You can purchase some fresh ginger root at your local grocery and refrigerate it, or you can purchase it dried. It is excellent for relieving nausea and settling upset stomachs. You can make a ginger tea by steeping 4 to 5 slices in boiled water for 10 to 15 min. Dr. Yamoda, M.D., from Tokyo shares this:

- A hot ginger compress can relieve muscular aches and pains, joint stiffness, abdominal cramps and a stiff neck. Bring a gallon of distilled or spring water to a boil in a large pot (preferably not aluminum) with a lid on top. Wash 1-1/2 fresh ginger roots, but don't peel them.

---

1. http://tinyurl.com/GarlicEarDrops

Grate the root by rotating clockwise instead of back and forth as the root fibers are tough and this method will keep the fibers from clogging the grater. Put the ginger root in a clean muslin or cotton cloth and tie with a string. Turn off the water and place the cloth bag into it, squeezing the juice from the bag into the water.

- Let it steep for seven more minutes. Press the bag against the sides of the pot with a wooden spoon to turn the water yellow. Use this water for compresses that should be applied rather hot without scalding the skin. Use a terry washcloth or two—dipped into the pot and gently rung out into the pot. The steaming towel is folded to fit the particular area of the skin. Place a second compress on the same area or slightly next to it. Then place a large folded towel over all to retain most of the heat. Keep on for 15 to 20 minutes. Repeat again in 4 to 6 hours as needed.[1]

Homeopathic remedy: Carbo Vegetabilis 12C - 30C

Indicated for people who have mild digestive problems such as dyspepsia and flatulence (gas), especially after eating fatty foods or drinking wine. Dosage: Five pellets as needed.

Capsule: Charcoal

Take one capsule to relieve flatulence as needed. (See also Flu Symptoms/ Charcoal below.) It is very absorbing.

Fever

Fever is the body's primary mechanism for fighting disease. Allowing a moderate fever to run its course may reduce the length of time you'll be sick. If the person is having trouble sleeping and resting, give an adult aspirin or Tylenol to reduce the fever. If the fever does not come down after 24 hours or it rises above 104°F, *immediately* cool the patient by washing him/her with cold water or rubbing alcohol and get medical help. Keep children's aspirin or Tylenol in your First-Aid kit.

Flu

- **Prevention:** During flu season, wash your hands frequently with warm water and soap. Avoid shaking hands or touching your eyes and mouth. Cough into your elbow.

---

1. Heinerman

- **Symptoms:** Flu comes on quickly; nose is congested, with possible headache, sore throat, muscle aches, and chills/fever. You may be sensitive to light and be very tired. Cough may be severe and lingering.

For best results, take any herbal or homeopathic remedies as soon as you feel a cold or flu coming on, and follow the directions. If you delay, the cold will have you for about seven days, no matter what you do.

Homeopathic Remedy: Gelsemium Sempervirens 30C

For flu-like symptoms with overall weakness, shivering, stiffness and heaviness of the limbs and headaches that radiate into the neck and shoulders. A person will not be thirsty. Dosage: 5 pellets 4 times a day.

Homeopathic remedy: Oscillococcinum

For flu symptoms: mild fever, chills, body aches and pains. It is best to take this as soon as symptoms appear, and repeat 1 or 2 times at 6-hour intervals. If the illness has already developed, take 1 dose 2 times daily. Dosage: These will come in packages with directions on the packet.

Herb: Charcoal

We have friends who, along with others, developed an unusual bacterial infection in their legs while overseas. Those who took several capsules of charcoal got well almost a week ahead of those who did not. We also know of people whose upset stomachs cleared up rapidly after eating burnt toast.

Frostbite

Frostbite is similar to a skin burn and often appears on cheeks, nose, ears, fingers and toes. It is a condition where the skin and sometimes deeper tissues are actually frozen. First Aid: Seek medical help if you can.

- **Symptoms:** Initially the area may have a painful pin-prick sensation, which will then turn cold, hard and numb. It can occur suddenly, especially if the skin is exposed and it is windy. Visual signs are splotchy, opaque, pale, and yellowish-white areas on exposed skin. Cover these areas if you can't get out of the cold.

- **Treatment:** Enter a warm area. Remove all tight clothing, including boots and socks. Clothing that has frozen onto the body should be thawed by immersion in warm water, but *avoid damaging any frozen skin.* Begin warming the frostbitten parts by immersion in water (temperature 100°F, 38°C). If warm water is not available, expose the body to warm air, but not directly to an open fire. *Do not massage or rub the frostbitten parts of the body.* Give the person hot drinks or soup, but no alcohol. Do not prick or break any blisters. Do not aggressively move the injured extremities.

Headaches

If you are prone to headaches, you will obviously keep handy an over-the-counter drug of your choice.

Food: Basil

Take a level tsp. of dried, ground basil and put it into 1 cup of hot water for 10 min., then strain. When cooled, add 2 tbsp. of tincture of witch hazel that has been refrigerated, and apply this as a compress to the forehead and temples.[1]

Heat Cramps

Heat cramps come from an excessive loss of salt from the body, following exposure to heat.
- **Symptoms:** Severe cramps in the limbs, back and/or abdomen. The body temperature will remain normal.
- **Treatment:** Move the patient to a cool, shaded place. Remove the outer clothing, elevate the feet and move the legs up and down or massage the legs, or both. Give as much saline-water solution to the patient as they desire:

Saline Water Mixture:

1 tsp. of salt per pint of water to drink.

Heat Exhaustion

In hot climates excessive sweating causes dehydration and loss of salt. Vomiting, diarrhea or the use of alcohol can cause loss of body fluids, which increases the potential for heat exhaustion.
- **Symptoms:** Loss of appetite, dizziness. Cool, clammy sweating skin, listlessness. Nausea and vomiting, mild muscular cramps and pale skin. The heart may race and the person may have trouble concentrating. The temperature may be slightly below or above normal.
- **Treatment:** Keep the patient in a cool, well-ventilated area. Loosen and wet the clothing. Give the patient a saline-water solution. The person should rest for 24 hours while continuing to drink the solution.

---

1. Heinerman

Heat Stroke

Heat stroke can occur after a few hours in intense heat, but it normally occurs after a few days or weeks of exposure.

- **Symptoms:** The skin is dry, flushed and burning. Sweating has stopped. The person appears feverish, with a lack of coordination. There can be nausea, vomiting, restlessness and mental confusion. The person will have a headache. Respiration rate can rise; the pulse rate can be as high as 160/min.; twitching and cramps of the muscles will occur; Body temperature can be between 105°F (40°C) and 110°F (43°C); and delirium, collapse, convulsions and coma can lead to death.

- **Treatment:** Immediately cool the patient any way you can. It is very important to continually monitor the falling temperature of the patient, as exposure to cold might cause hypothermia. The temperature of the patient should be lowered to below 100°F (38°C).

- **Method:** move the patient to a cool place and remove all clothing. Cover the body with wet sheets, towels or whatever you can find and massage the person vigorously with a cold cloth and ice cubes if available. If you have access to a fan, direct the air flow over the wet sheets. If other persons are available, they can fan the body as well, with whatever is available. Immerse the person in a cold bath, stream, or a tub of ice-cold water. The body should begin sweating again at 100°F (38°C). Keep the patient in a cool place and watch for any signs of hypothermia. Continue to monitor the patient until he or she is stable. Get medical help if possible.

Have the patient drink a saline-water mixture (page 95) or fruit juice (use caution for diabetics). The patient should have 8 pints of the saline-water mixture or other fluids in the next 24 hours. When the patient is recovered, he/she should be covered with a light, dry blanket and be kept in a cool spot for a week, while continuing to drink a lot of water.

Hypothermia

- **Symptoms:** Victim feels cold and must move about to stay warm. Victim begins shivering and feeling numb. Shivering becomes uncontrollable. Speaking becomes difficult, thinking unclear. Muscles stiffen, and movements become jerky. Victim becomes sluggish and irrational. Victim becomes unresponsive. Heart and lungs cease operating.

- **Treatment:** Get the victim into a warm area. Remove wet clothing and replace with dry, warm clothes. Offer warm non-alcoholic drinks, if victim is conscious. Keep the victim awake. Warm the victim's trunk with hot-water bottles, hot bath, *etc.* Keep victim immobile until body temperature is normal.

Kidney Infection

Symptoms can include scant and cloudy urine that also contains pus; burning painful urination; pain in the back and groin; foul-smelling urine; high fever up to 104°F; and chills, nausea, vomiting, and severe headache. Seek medical care and keep flushing your system with water.

Menstrual Cramps and other Mild Stomach Cramping

Homeopathic Remedy: Colocynthis 12C

Indicated for mild abdominal pains of a cramp-like nature usually relieved by doubling over or by pressure and warmth, *e.g.* menstrual pains (person is irritable or angry), colicky pains associated with diarrhea, *etc.* Dosage: 5 pellets at time of pain.

Homeopathic remedy: Belladonna 30C

Use this remedy if you are suffering acute pain that begins and ends suddenly. Cramps may feel like labor pains, with intense weight and pressure in lower abdomen and pelvis. Dosage: 5 pellets every 2 hrs.

Herb: Peppermint

Because peppermint has an antispasmodic ability, a tea made of peppermint can also relieve cramps. It comes dried, fresh or in tea bags.

See also Ginger for cramps on page 88.

Migraines

30 million Americans get migraines, three-fourths of them women. Causes include menstrual cycles, alcohol, weather changes, stress, food, and sleep deprivation. These home remedies work for some people:
  • Drink water, as dehydration can cause headaches.
  • Drink caffeine to restrict blood vessels, and lessen pain, but caffeine may trigger headaches for heavy users of caffeine.
  • Tie a headband around the head.
  • Fish oil reduces inflammation and restricts the blood vessels in your temples.
  • Rub peppermint oil on the part of your head that hurts.

- Eat ginger or take ginger capsules to reduce nausea.
- Magnesium, in doses of 400 to 600 mg. per day, is effective for men-strual-associated migraines and those associated with auras, but may cause diarrhea.
- Vitamin B2 (Riboflavin) in doses of 400 mg. a day, can prevent migraines, but it causes some people to urinate more frequently or have darker urine, so the dosage may have to be adjusted.
- CoEnzymeQ10 in doses of 300 mg. per day reduces head pain.
- Cold (or hot) compress,[1] one may work better than another for you.

Herb: Feverfew

This is one of the few herbs that has been scientifically tested, and in clinical trials 7 out of 10 patients taking feverfew reported that their migraine headaches were less frequent, less painful or both. This herb can be purchased at health-food stores.

Mosquito Bites, Prevention and Treatment

Here are some guidelines from shamanic practitioner Gwilda Wiyaka's book[2] that can make yourself less palatable to insects.

- Food: Eating artificial food gives your skin an artificial aroma, which will make you attractive to mosquitoes, so eat natural, organic foods.
- Scents: Chemicals and perfumes in products that you wear, carry, or apply to yourself also mark you as mosquito food, so select products that are all natural and either unscented or scented with essential oils. Other insects are also drawn to scents.
- Smoke conceals your scent and repels mosquitoes, so waft some over your body when you are outside, preferably fire smoke.
- Attitude: Fear and avoidance emit frequencies that mark you as mosquito food, so rather than thinking, "Oh, please, don't bite me," think, "I am not the food you seek." The more at home in nature you feel, the less you appear as prey.
- Boosting your immune system through natural supplementation can not only prevent your getting bitten, but it can also keep you from becoming sick, should a mosquito slip through and bite you.

---

1. http://tinyurl.com/MigraineRemedies
2. http://tinyurl.com/WiyakaBook

- Bite treatment: If you live in an area with West Nile Virus: Take a warm bath of Epsom salts (1 cup per tub) to draw out the foreign properties that cause disease, then apply a poultice of clay and apple-cider vinegar to the bites to continue the rebalancing process and reduce your chances of getting sick.

Essential Oil: Peppermint

Apply peppermint essential oil to relieve the itching.

Repellents for Mosquitoes and other Pesky Biting Bugs

While you are at the health-food store, pick up some natural, essential-oil-based insect repellent like Burt's Bees Herbal Insect Repellent, Buzz Away or Natural Herbal Armor. Understand, however, that many of the natural chemicals used in herbal repellents are highly volatile and evaporate quickly, so they need more frequent application, rarely lasting more than three hours. You might also purchase some clove essential oil to add to the formula for extra protection, but never apply it directly on your skin, as it will burn. Mix it with a neutral oil, before applying it to your skin.

Oil of lemon eucalyptus, sold as Citriodiol (no relation to citronella), is one of the few natural-based repellents that has been proven effective at repelling insects for six hours or more. It is in brands such as Repel, Cutter and Coleman Botanicals.

You may want to concoct your own repellent from essential oils. Here is a recipe from Young Living Essential Oils:[1]

- 3 drops lavender
- 4 drops geranium
- 3 drops eucalyptus
- 2 drops lemon
- 1 drop peppermint
- 1 drop clove

As a daily body wash, Avon's Skin So Soft™ Moisturizing Shower Gel[2] effectively discourages insect bites all day long. The other products in that line repel insects, too. Wearing long, loose and light-colored clothing outside, especially during dusk and dawn, is also good advice.

---

1. http://tinyurl.com/YoungLivingRepellentRecipe
2. http://tinyurl.com/SSSshowerGel

Muscle Pulls, Strains, Tendon Pulls, Aches and Pains

If the injury is severe or minor, first remember RICE: Rest, Ice, Compress and Elevate. Follow your first-aid advice and, if it is a major injury, seek medical care, if available.

Homeopathic Remedy: Arnica Montana 3C to 30C

Eases the pain from simple sprains, pulled tendons, pain and stiffness, strains, bruising and muscular aches. Dosage: Five pellets every 30 min., up to 10 doses. Decrease with improvement. This also comes in a cream form.

Nausea And Vomiting

First and foremost allow your stomach to release the irritant—it is the body's mechanism for removing toxins. Dehydration is critical to watch after vomiting. Sip water to see when your body is ready to hold it down. As it begins staying down, drink more. Move to clear broths and add bland foods when you are ready.

Homeopathic remedy: Ipecacuanha 12C

For symptoms of nausea, vomiting, mild diarrhea, and hyper-salivation with a clear, non-coated tongue. Dosage: 5 pellets 2 to 4 times a day, depending on the severity of symptoms.

Nose Bleeds, Menstrual Bleeding

Herb: Witch Hazel

Apply distilled witch hazel to the nasal passages with a cotton ball and apply a cold compress to the back of the neck.

Note: if the nose is bleeding from a blow to the head, it could be a sign of a fractured skull. Seek medical help.

Homeopathic remedy: Phosphorus 6C

For people who tend to bleed easily and experience frequent nosebleeds, bleeding gums, or heavy menstrual periods. Dosage: Five pellets every 6 hours. For a nosebleed brought on by blowing the nose, the dosage is: 5 pellets every 2 min., up to 10 doses.

Nuclear Radiation Poisoning

Seek medical care. Radiation is invisible. You may not see anything.

Symptoms: reddened skin, nausea, vomiting, diarrhea, fatigue, and loss of hair and appetite.

What to do: Tune into your radio; find out what's happening and where the radioactive plume is heading. Determine whether and how to evacuate (see page 34). If it's coming your way, grab your *Go Pack* and get out of the way, evacuating at right angles.

Poison, Ingesting

If you suspect that someone has ingested poisonous household materials, call the Poison Help Line at 1-800-222-1222, which offers free, confidential medical advice for all poisons 24 hours a day, seven days a week, unless the phones are down, in which case try to remove materials from the victim's mouth, turn him on his side, and follow directions on the product's label, if you can find the container.

Poison Ivy and Poison Oak: See Rashes, below

Skin Issues: Rashes

Food: Carrots

Many folk healers believe that almost any itching and burning of the skin can be eased with a carrot poultice. Scrub the carrot well, but do not peel. Finely grate it onto a clean cloth and apply to the affected area.

Herb: Goldenseal

If you have capsules, dissolve one to two capsules in 6 to 8 oz. of warm water. If you have powder, take 1 tsp. in 6 to 8 oz. of warm water. Use this cooled mixture to dab on the afflicted parts of the skin.

Wild Plant: Yarrow

Make a tea from the plant's leaves, stem and/or flowers and apply the liquid to rashes, skin ulcers and hemorrhoids.

Wild Plant: Jewelweed

Jewelweed often grows near poison ivy or streams, and is a natural antidote to poison ivy. Crush the stem and leaves, then rub the gel-like liquid into the skin contacted by the poison ivy, and the symptoms will not appear or will be reduced. Jewelweed is also effective on poison oak, okra spines, stinging nettle, bug bites, razor burn, acne, heat rash, ringworm and other skin disorders. A poultice made from it is an old folk remedy used for bruises, burns, cuts, eczema, insect bites, sores, sprains, warts, and ringworm. Check it out in your plant book if it grows near you.

Wild Plant: Red Clover

Making a tea from the flowers of red clover and applying to the affected area can relieve eczema and psoriasis.

Extract: Calendula

Calendula is an antiseptic and antibacterial herb. We recommend that you buy it in extract form. Apply it directly to the skin, but not during pregnancy.

Sore Throats

Herb: Goldenseal (powder, capsule or extract)

It can be used in a mouthwash or gargle for infected gums and canker sores as well as sore throats. Mix about 1/2 tsp. with 8 oz. of boiled water.

Herbal Extract: Echinacea

Tonsillitis, inflamed gums: dissolve at least one dropperful of extract into warm water and gargle and/or rinse your mouth out.

Household Solution: Table Salt

Mix 1 tsp. salt to 8 oz. of lukewarm water. It is an excellent gargle for sore throats. You can also combine this with a small amount of apple-cider vinegar.

Supplement: Zinc

Zinc lozenges or pills can be the first line of defense against colds and sore throats. To gargle with it, crush a pill in water. *Caution:* it may cause nausea when taken on an empty stomach, therefore take it with food.

Ticks: How To Remove

Apply some liquid soap to a cotton ball. Cover the tick with the soap-soaked cotton ball and swab it for 15 to 20 seconds. The tick will come out on its own. Insect body parts left inside your skin may become infected.

Early symptoms of Lyme Disease: Rash. A small, red bump may appear at the site of the bite, which is normal and does not indicate Lyme disease. If the redness expands over a few days, forming a bull's-eye rash pattern, with a red outer ring surrounding a clear area, seek immediate medical treatment, for this is one of the hallmarks of Lyme disease. You can also experience flu-like symptoms—fever, chills, fatigue, body aches and a headache.

Toothaches

Essential Oil: Peppermint or Spearmint Oil

Apply a few drops directly to the sore tooth and gums. If you do not have the oil, gently chew on some leaves.

Food: Cloves

Most of us have cloves in our spice cabinets. Cloves can be used as a temporary toothache anesthetic. Chew gently around the tooth.

Wild Plant: Yarrow

If you have Yarrow growing nearby and have carefully identified it, you can chew on some leaves, which will lessen the pain of a toothache.

Yeast Infections

Herb: Goldenseal

Mix a solution of 3 cups of water (preferably non-chlorinated) with 1.5 tsps. of powdered goldenseal. Douche with this several times a day until the condition clears. This infection is a sign that your pH balance is acidic and that your diet needs to come back into balance.

"The ideal diet for those suffering from Candida yeast overgrowth is to eat a diet high in fiber and protein complimented by some complex carbohydrates and a small amount of fresh fruits. For example, the daily intake should be approximately: 65% high-fiber foods, such as steamed vegetables. The best choices are broccoli, celery, radishes, asparagus, onions, garlic, ginger root, cabbage, turnips and kale. Raw garlic and onions act as natural anti-fungal substances and should be eaten as much as possible."[1]

1. http://tinyurl.com/CandidaYeastInfect

13

Community

EVERYTHING YOU NEED TO KNOW, YOU LEARNED FROM NOAH'S ARK...
NOAH DID NOT GO IT ALONE.

Before 9/11/2001, many people described New York City as an uncaring and cold place, where few made eye contact for fear of being targeted, and where many people you met were gruff and rushed. But, during and after the emergency, New Yorkers showed their true mettle and reached out to others in need, regardless of race, creed, economic status or political persuasion. We saw the same phenomenon on display in Boston after the Marathon bombings—people help one another. It is something we can depend on.

TIP
HARD TIMES SHARED ARE HALF AS HARD,
WHILE GOOD TIMES SHARED ARE TWICE THE FUN.

Those who live through tough times are changed forever, and your life may be changed, too, when it is time to face whatever is on *your* path.

DEPENDING ON EACH OTHER

Our great nation was founded on the principles of individualism and freedom, ideals that have always been augmented by the power of coordinated effort. Individual colonists could not dislodge the British Army until they found the collective power to improve their situation, which is still true today. Most loners sooner or later succumb to challenges that are better faced with friends. Infants without human touch die. Some of us think that we can survive alone, but the real truth is that for long-term survival, we really need each other.

TIP
YOU ARE MORE LIKELY TO SURVIVE WITH THE HELP OF OTHERS THAN ON YOUR OWN. DO NOT LET YOUR PRIDE THREATEN YOUR FAMILY'S SURVIVAL.

We no longer live in tribes, but we do live in groups that serve as tribes. If you have not completed the assembly of your *Go Pack* or *Stash* by the time you need them, you can turn to your friends as a potential source for missing items. You may have extra lighters, for example, which you might barter for a friend's extra compass. Give close friends a copy of this book as a gift, and discuss the issues inside it with them. See who is aware enough of the challenges to prepare ahead of time, and then develop stronger ties to them.

Wherever you are, communication is essential in maintaining community ties. We have made it clear that cell phones are almost indispensable in today's unpredictable world, and we have stressed the significance of keeping important cell-phone numbers and email addresses with your emergency supplies, on paper and in your *Go Pack*, for when all else fails.

> Emergency numbers:
> See page 143.
>
> Friends' Skills &
> Resources:
> See page 154.

During emergencies cell phones may not work, so be ready to do without. Remember that old-fashioned plug-in-the-wall phones work without power. Word spreads fast these days, so you can trust that even if you are completely cut off, someone may have seen you, or there are others in your same situation. In a crisis, people act together.

Some innovative local governments are using the Internet to set up local self-reliance emergency-response web sites. Individuals log on to the local site at the first indication of an emergency, and the pertinent emergency instructions are posted there, including automatic posting of current wind speed and direction. These sites also serve as a communications exchange on the local level, building a community of people who can barter with each other and find other local people with skills and knowledge that they need.

You might want to consider making a Facebook page for your network of friends on whom you could rely during an emergency, but remember that the Internet could be down during an emergency, so you'll be relying on your paper list with contact information (see page 154).

TIP

LEARN TO TWEET ON YOUR CELL PHONE.[1] IT CAN BE A LIFE LINE.

TWITTER

For those of you rare folks who do not use Twitter regularly—and we know you are out there—here is some help on a good Internet tool. Twitter is a widely used service over smart phones and computers that circulates short text messages of up to 140 characters. During Sandy, New Jersey drivers tweeted using the #njgas hashtag. Other tweeters, finding gas or its price or absence, were sharing the information for all to see. During the San Diego, Calif., forest fires of 2007, the

---

1. http://tinyurl.com/Twitter-Hash-How

hashtag "#sandiegofire" identified updates related to the disaster. During the Fukushima earthquake and tsunami of April, 2011, most communications were out of service, but text messages and tweets mostly got through. In Arab countries, many activists who played crucial roles in the Arab Spring used social networking as a key tool to express their thoughts concerning unjust acts committed by their governments. One Egyptian Arab Spring activist explained, "We use Facebook to schedule the protests, Twitter to coordinate, and YouTube to tell the world."[1]

HOW TO TWEET DURING AN EMERGENCY

Using Twitter

1. Sign up for Twitter and select an @ID.[1]

2. Learn how to use Twitter.[2]

3. Make a hashtag at any time simply by typing a phrase of the form "#topic" into a tweet. Then, other Tweeters can use that hashtag in their own tweets to add to the larger conversation about that topic.

4. If something is going on, people you follow will be tweeting about it, and there will be hashtags in those tweets. Find out what hashtags are trending.[3]

5. Clicking a blue hashtag sends you to that hashtag's page, where you will see other tweets using that hashtag.

Click "Top" to see tweets with the hashtag that have been retweeted numerous times, or "All" tweets that include the hashtag.

1. http://tinyurl.com/TweetHowToSignUp
2. http://tinyurl.com/TweetHowTo
3. http://tinyurl.com/TweetTrends

Keep your messages short, clear, and specific. Leave out the details, for they take battery life. You can create your own hashtags, so use hashtags that emergency responders might search for. Town names and roads or intersections are good, and forget punctuation.

Gather the Twitter IDs of local emergency response agencies, news outlets, or other relevant people or organizations, so you can include them in your tweets as so-called "@ replies" to get their attention. They might retweet or otherwise pass along your messages to officials.

Here are real examples of well-structured emergency tweets:
• Power outages: No power Prescott neighborhood Oakland @pge4me

• Injuries: Collapsed apt bldg 40th & Simpson Greenville. 2 trapped, hurt @jingville

1. http://tinyurl.com/Twitter-FB-YouTube

- Extensive damages: 600 block 14th St. Berkeley 10+ houses destroyed @insidebayarea

Twitter is a great survival tool for this modern age. It creates temporary "hashtag communities" on the fly, as needed, and it saves lives. Learn it, if you can. When an emergency strikes, with the Internet, you are not alone. As long as the Internet is up, you can share information and ideas

USHAHIDI

Ushahidi is a web and mobile platform that allows individuals to create, visualize and share stories on a map. It allows people to share their stories on their own terms, using the tools they already have. It is free and open-source software, so anyone can get involved in using or developing it.[1] It was initially developed collaboratively by Kenyan citizen journalists to map reports of violence there in 2008. The original website mapped

Ushahidi on smart phone.
Credit: GlobalEnvision.org

incidents of violence and peace efforts throughout the country, based on reports submitted via the web and mobile phones.

The service was also used during the earthquakes in Haiti and Chile in 2010. Now it has become a global phenomenon in use around the planet, wherever people need to react to crises.[2]

During the revolution in Syria, Ushahidi has been coordinating response efforts to aid refugees, enabling them to escape the fighting. Its documentation of killings throughout the nation

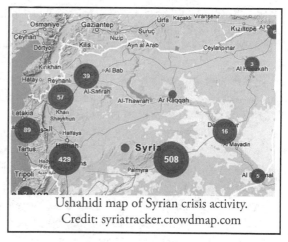

Ushahidi map of Syrian crisis activity.
Credit: syriatracker.crowdmap.com

allowed the world to see clearly what was happening in Syria.

---

1. http://community.ushahidi.com
2. http://tinyurl.com/CrisisMgt

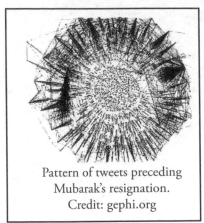

Pattern of tweets preceding
Mubarak's resignation.
Credit: gephi.org

The technology is even beginning to predict oncoming flash points by mapping in real time the patterns of tweets in an area of concern.[1]

This image is the visual representation of Twitter traffic with the hashtag #jan25 on February 11, 2011, when President Hosni Mubarak's resignation was announced. If you used this hashtag, or retweeted someone who did, or your tweet with this hashtag was retweeted, your username might be one of these tiny points.

VIRTUAL COMMUNITY

Crowdsourcing is the practice of obtaining needed services, ideas, or content by soliciting contributions from a large group of people, especially from the online community rather than from traditional employees or suppliers.

About dinner time on July 14, 2011, torrential rain in Mumbai was clogging roads when several bombs went off around the city. With telephone lines jammed, people used social networks to post their whereabouts and seek those of their loved ones. Facebook became a discussion forum. Tweeters exchanged important real-time updates. Moments after the explosions, an editable Google Docs[2] spreadsheet was created by an IT engineer 720 miles away. The link to it began circulating via Twitter, carrying names, addresses and phone numbers of people offering their houses as refuges to stranded people. The link was retweeted to help funnel missed phone numbers from stale Twitter messages onto a single page, which registered hundreds of entries. It showed that online response to a crisis can be highly disciplined.

A half-hour after the blast, a vacationing software engineer 750 miles away started a disaster-tracker map on Ushahidi. Using hashtags such as #here2help, #needhelp and #MumbaiBlasts, the engineer flagged the map of Mumbai, indicating where people were stranded, or where they could seek shelter. Color-coded dots on the map linked people to traffic updates, death tolls, blood donors, hospital phone numbers, *etc.* When he became swamped by the inflow of data, he sought and received help from volunteers.

---

1. Video http://tinyurl.com/MubaricTwitterPattern
2. https://accounts.google.com

People are prepared to go to great lengths collectively to ensure that critical information that is available via social media is reliable, which flies in the face of Mark Twain's quip that a lie can travel halfway around the world while truth is putting on its shoes—a problem that, one might imagine, is only exacerbated by the media like Twitter. Instead, it appears that responsible netizens co-operate to stop rumors in their tracks and focus instead on re-tweeting important information. When a hoaxed tweet sank the stock market April 23, 2013, social media uncovered the hoax within five minutes, and the market quickly recovered. Social platforms show just how much good can be achieved, often in a few characters, when people use them prudently.

COMMUNICATION

Information about what is happening elsewhere is essential to survival and can be traded for other needed things. An important item in your *Stash* is a battery-powered, solar-powered or hand-cranked AM/FM (or best—shortwave) radio. If it is battery powered, make sure you have backup batteries and change them twice yearly when daylight savings time changes. Radio Shack carries an FRX3 Hand Turbine AM/FM Weather Radio with Smartphone Charger for about $60[1] that can keep your portable devices charged by hand-cranking or solar power. If the electrical grid is down, your smart phone will not be smart very long without a way to charge it. See page 27 for USB chargers that run on wood or sun. A National Weather Service All Hazard Weather Radio is recommended. You can find them in grocery stores now, for $30 or so. Be sure to call 888-697-7263 to set it up before you need it.

TIP
NOAA WEATHER RADIO FREQUENCIES
162.4, 162.425, 162.45, 162.475, 162.5, 162.525, 162.55

Four Scenarios

AWAY FROM HOME, WITHOUT A VEHICLE

Unless you are experiencing an individual event, it is likely that those around you are in the same fix you are, so form the bonds of crisis with others. If you are in a unique fix, call 911 on your cell phone, and help will come.

---

1. http://tinyurl.com/WR-111B

AWAY FROM HOME, IN YOUR VEHICLE

If you are stuck with other vehicles nearby, those bonds of crisis will come in handy. Use your *Vehicle Box* and your *Go Pack* to help others in need. If you are alone in your vehicle, away from others, use your cell phone to call for help and talk with loved ones. Use the radio to keep you company and keep you informed. A book stored in your vehicle can help pass the time. It's a good idea to keep a versatile phone charger in your vehicle. (See page 27.)

STUCK AT HOME, NO UTILITIES

Friends Skills & Resource List: See page 154.

You never have to know or have everything, if you know someone who knows or has what you need when you need it. Start now to assess the skills and resources of your neighbors and close-by friends that may be useful in an emergency and make a list that you can all refer to later when the need arises. Keep the list current and store a copy in your *Go Pack* and another with your *Stash*.

EVACUATED FROM HOME

If you have time, coordinate with trusted friends who are prepared, and plan to evacuate with them where possible. There is safety in numbers. Don't delay for anyone, but rather go when you need to, with those who are ready to accompany you. Arrange with family members as to where to meet in case of an emergency and select different places for different situations.

Use the form on page 153 to discuss meeting arrangements in different situations. Make sure everyone has consistent information on rendezvous sites.

TIP

MAKE SURE YOUR FAMILY KNOWS WHERE YOU MIGHT GO.

The Internet is a virtual community that can be useful in many ways, like assembling a network of like-minded folks to support each other during emergencies. If, for example, a nuclear meltdown forces a vast region to be evacuated, perhaps permanently, it would be most valuable to have assembled beforehand a set of friends in various regions who could put you up for a while, providing that you make the same offer to them.

TIP

LEARN HOW TO ACCESS YOUR EMAIL VIA PUBLIC-ACCESS POINTS
SUCH AS LIBRARIES AND CYBERCAFÉS, IN CASE YOU NEED TO.

Keep your friends' current cell phone and email addresses in the "Friends' Skills and Resources" table on page 154, and encourage them to do the same with yours. When your cell-phone battery is dead, paper is a good thing.

BARTER AND MONEY

"Money is a good that acts as a medium of exchange in transactions."[1]

Money developed as a way to make barter more efficient. That is all that money is. Barter is the exchange of resources or services for mutual advantage, a practice over 10,000 years old. But it was not convenient. Perhaps a digger has an extra shovel but needs shoes, while a shoemaker has a shovel but needs bread, and a farmer has bread and shoes but needs a shovel. Then, somebody is always missing at the critical moment. So people found things of common value to exchange, like cattle, which could provide food and leather. Soon rare and beautiful cowrie shells were traded, then bronze and copper imitation cowrie shells, precious-metal coins, paper money, and finally theoretical money, in the form of digital strings of bits in computers.

Stored food (see page 57) not only can keep you alive for a while, but you can trade it with neighbors for exchange of resources or services to your mutual advantage. You can get a 12-meal food planning pack for $15 or so, from efoods.com, and it lasts 25 years. Having some of these around would be valuable barter items.

Bartering is not only cost-effective, but it also helps build trust, which is always important. Bartering is often best done in person, but it can also be done effectively online[2],[3] at several sites.

In most countries of the world, barter is second nature, but not in the US, therefore getting accustomed to bartering will allow you to feel more comfortable doing it when it is really needed. Consider bartering to fill out your *Go Pack* (page 145) and *Stash* lists (page 148).

---

1. http://tinyurl.com/Money-Definition
2. http://www.tradeaway.com
3. http://tinyurl.com/10BestBarterSites

14

Our Greater Connection

*EVERYTHING YOU NEED TO KNOW, YOU LEARNED FROM NOAH'S ARK...
NO MATTER THE STORM, WHEN YOU HAVE FAITH,
THERE'S ALWAYS A RAINBOW WAITING.*

SPIRITUAL STOCKPILING

In the item checklists for your *Go Pack* and *Stash*, you might have noticed an odd listing, "items, sacred," with a high-priority assignment. It is not for us to tell you what that would be, but you'll know. For some it will be a Bible, for others a Buddhist icon or a Native American medicine bag. It is what you reach for to confirm your connection with the Sacred.

Another item you will find there is "photos of loved ones." It again has a high priority, because of its value to you in certain situations, and the low cost and little space it takes. In times of great disasters, it is good to have loved ones near by, but if they aren't, pictures are the next best thing. How often do we see people searching through the rubble of their former home for pictures? Keep copies of your favorite photos in water-tight baggies. Wet photos are dissapointing. Many of us have pictures stored on computers, or in the cloud, but paper prints require no power.

FACING CRISES

When we are in a crisis, we look for something greater than ourselves, and we look to those things that mean the most to us. This will be different for everyone, and it is whoever or whatever makes you feel the most supported—your spiritual community, family or friends—and these are the people you can work with to prepare for the unexpected.

"God helps those who help themselves" is our philosophy. Don't run in fear, but carefully prepare for the unexpected disaster. When we are prepared, we can move through danger with the confidence that we've done all we can, and now it's up to our own instincts and faith to get us through. There is only so much we can control, so look to what you *can* control and prepare in the best way. Preparation may make the difference between smoothly moving through a disaster versus encountering extraordinary difficulties.

Faith in the will to live is one of our most powerful human gifts. It gets us more easily through very difficult times. It can help us be found under tons of rubble; it can help us survive many days under a ruined building until help comes; it can help us walk miles and survive unbelievable cold, wind, rain and hunger. It is an invaluable aspect of being human that you carry with you.

Science changed dramatically 100 years ago with the discovery of the quantum field, and while mainstream science is still absorbing its implications, new science is applying quantum mechanics to living systems and changing the way we see the world. Briefly, quantum physics tells us that human consciousness affects the sub-atomic particles connecting our mind and physical matter.[1] In other words, our thoughts, powered by feelings, *really do* create our perceived reality.

This understanding of science gives new meaning to the power of positive thinking, and it explains otherwise unexplainable events.

THE POWER WE HAVE

In San Diego in 1979, *e.g.*, a 5-foot-3, 116-pound woman lifted a 4,500-pound Cadillac off of an eight-year-old girl who was trapped under its wheel. The child was treated and released from the hospital. The woman lifted the car, because she knew that if she did, it would save the girl. So she put the *thought* in her mind and *deeply felt* that she could; and she did. This is just one example of how profoundly powerful we all are. There are many stories like this.

We strive to keep a positive attitude about our life and what we draw into it, and now we understand through quantum mechanics how important that is, because that's how the universe works. Our thoughts and feelings define our lives, so we might as well choose to keep an upbeat attitude and see a bright future coming, because we can have it either way.

Taking on all the tasks we suggest in this book could seem daunting, since we all have such busy lives these days, so each week set a goal to become prepared on one or two items, and before you know it, you will be ready.

Then...if a crisis does come, you are better prepared to get through it with confidence, ingenuity, and resilience. If no disaster comes, you are blessed. Use your stored food in rotation, use your *Go Pack* on picnics and hikes, and enjoy life!

---

1. Bennett

Section III
Understanding Weirdness

15

That Uncertainty in the Air

EVERYTHING YOU NEED TO KNOW, YOU LEARNED FROM NOAH'S ARK...
SOMETIMES IT RAINS MORE THAN YOU EXPECT,
AND LATER THINGS ARE FOREVER CHANGED.

Every day, we make assumptions about how our environment and society will provide us and our families with safety, food, water, warmth and shelter. And yet, with every passing day, these assumptions seem to be coming unglued. Meteors come out of the sky. The water often tastes bad. Lights go out. Too many children get cancer. Is this a pattern that can be expected to continue, or is it just a long sequence of coincidences of no particular meaning? In order to make good decisions, we need to understand what is going on. Without such understanding, we cannot see what is coming, and we are blind in some sense, as these historical examples illustrate:

On October 12, 1492, Taino natives along the shore of what is now San Salvador looked up to see three overly large canoes. Their world had changed.

Centuries later, the owner of a buggy-whip factory awoke to see the streets filled with horseless carriages. His world had changed.

One night the captain of a whaling ship full of premium whale oil for lamps sailed into home port to see his city glittering with electric lights. His world had changed.

Eastman Kodak Co., the once-mighty photographic-equipment, printing, and imaging company, awoke one day to see people using digital cameras. Its annual sales dropped sharply, and it lost a fortune. Despite Paul Simon's plea, "Don't take my Kodachrome away," Kodak's world had changed.

In India, in late July, 2012, 700 million people were suddenly plunged into darkness as their entire power grid shuddered and quit. Life without electricity for two days was not on their list of expectations that day. Trains stopped. Toll gates locked. Air conditioners were silent.

Americans have always felt that real estate was their best investment and that such investments would always increase in value—until 2008, when a sudden economic collapse not only caused housing prices to drop, but also caused many people to lose their homes.

After Katrina, many people had to relocate and restart their lives in brand-new cities. After folks in New Jersey experienced Sandy and then Winter Storm Athena, it took many months to begin to return to "normal." The area may never again be what it once was.

What had until then always been a festive time, the Boston Marathon of April 15, 2013, instantly became a scene of deadly chaos. People had assumed that great public celebrations were fun and safe environments.

In West, Tex., about 8:00 p.m. on April 17, 2013, Eleanor Castro, 76, was taking a shower in her home. She assumed that the experience would be warm and comforting and that she could soon relax for the evening. Instead, a massive explosion at an ammonium nitrate plant a mile and half away spun her around, knocking out power to her house. Fourteen people she knew lay still, and 200 more were injured. An entire small town was devastated in an instant.

What is common to all these tales is that what was assumed to be true one moment turned out to be false the next. Assumptions can be unreliable, and inflexibility can be dangerous in times of change.

The inflexible buggy-whip makers and whale-oil brokers no doubt went out of business. When one is heavily and inflexibly invested in a single way of doing things, it can be devastating when that one way is suddenly displaced by another. Those who walk away from underwater mortgages find rentals. Former Kodak employees seek other work. People who have gone through major disasters often rebuild, but their lives are forever changed.

There is a distinct possibility that many assumptions upon which we have built our castles may soon turn out to be quicksand. Traditionally, when people collide with failed assumptions, they react in predictable ways, most of which are unhelpful.

REACTION STYLES

- *Head in the Sand.* Here the operating assumption is that if one ignores a threat, it will not have to be dealt with. These people are like the captain of the Titanic who kept assuring everyone that everything would be all right, if only they would relax.

- *Denial.* At a time when NOAA announced that we have just come through the hottest year in history,[1] there are still those that cling to the idea that nothing has changed. These are like the people who rearranged sliding deck chairs as the Titanic was sinking.

---

1. http://tinyurl.com/2012hottestyear

- *Panic.* Run for your life! Every man for himself! Such people are like the captain of the Costa Concordia, who steered his huge vessel onto the rocks off of Italy and then beat everyone to the lifeboats.

So what can we do? We can choose a reaction style; but our philosophy is to be prepared for what you can expect, and expect the *unexpected.* The only certain thing is change, but we still too often proceed through life as if everything will remain as it was. However, uncertainty hangs in the air, like some societal floating anxiety. Change is happening faster than ever, and that bothers us. But, if we humans are anything, we are creative and adaptable. We will meet the challenges, and we will be better for it.

LIVING IN A COSMIC BOWLING ALLEY

The winter of 2013 saw a meteor explode over Russia, breaking 4,000 windows and injuring 1,100 people. On November 19, 2012, a massive coronal mass ejection (CME), larger than the Earth erupted from the Sun and tore through space away from us.[1] Again, on March 8, 2013, another enormous CME blew out of the sun, away from us. Had either hit our atmosphere, our communications satellites would likely have been fried, and all electrical grids and electronic devices would probably have failed on the side facing the sun.

We have chosen to use strings of electronic bits of 0's and 1's to determine what everyone's wealth is, what they owe others, and what others owe them, even what nations owe each other. Everything electronic is susceptible to disruption. In short, all of the valuations intrinsic in our economic system could be zeroed out by a solar flare. Furthermore, there would be no communication, no TV or radio, no cell phones. The society would be literally cold and dark, and the greatest economic engine of all time would be dead, and its confused citizens would be in deep shock. Solar flares are becoming more frequent and larger, and it seems that we are living in some kind of cosmic bowling alley, with shockingly large meteors raking our skies and asteroids passing between us and our communications satellites.

What can we do?

- We cannot prevent such things, but we have covered what to do if a minor cosmic event causes the power to fail, the phones to go down, or the utilities to become inoperable.

- If a major celestial object strikes the Earth, you will not be needing this book, and nothing we could say would make a difference.

---

1. Video http://tinyurl.com/CME-11-19-12

ASSUMPTIONS ABOUT NUCLEAR WAR

We assumed after the Cold War with Russia ended and agreements were made to reduce our nuclear weapons that we could close that ugly chapter in human history. However, nuclear proliferation and the probability of war in the Mideast (now also on the Korean Peninsula) are political issues that require attention at a high level, throughout the world, all the time. These issues are beyond the scope of this book, except that common sense submits that we as a species have arrived at the point where we need to speedily graduate past the use of war as a method of solving problems. Armed conflicts decide nothing; rather, they sow ever more seeds of future conflicts. The possibility that nuclear weapons could be used in *any* conflict should cause all of us to quickly conclude that war is now obsolete, unsustainable, and unaffordable on this planet. Common sense suggests that the sooner we get to a global consensus on this, the better chance our species will have to survive long-term.

> *Should mankind renounce war, or should we put an end to the human race?*
> —*The Russel/Einstein Manifesto 1955*

What can we do?

We can pray for sanity and common sense in our leaders and refer to "Our Greater Connection" on page 112.

ASSUMPTIONS ABOUT THE WEB OF LIFE

Our Place in It

The most basic assumption that most people will need to adopt, if we are to survive as a species on this planet, is that we *are* a species on this planet, *i.e.,* we are not *observers* of the Web of Life—we are *participants* in it.

As we have noted, for the first time in history, humankind is facing self-induced threats of very serious kind: Can our species survive long-term on this planet we have been fouling? In nature, a species that fouls its own nest does not survive long. According to a major study that compiled thousands of published reports,[1] our planet is undergoing its sixth major global extinction crisis, the first to be traced to a single species—*Homo sapiens*. Beyond reducing our individual footprints on the Earth, what can we do? Understanding our place in the world is the first step.

---

1. Ceballos

The populations and species of other organisms supply and maintain vital ecosystem services like flood control, carbon absorption, nutrient recycling, soil generation, crop pollination, and agricultural-pest control, so losing their services through extinction can threaten our very survival as a species. It is expected that climate change will greatly increase the rate of extinction, as species lose habitat. Biologist Edward O. Wilson has said that our causing this extinction crisis is "the folly our descendants are least likely to forgive us."[1]

The most numerous bird on Earth, the passenger pigeon, went extinct on September 1, 1914, when 29-year-old Martha fell off her perch and died. Only a century earlier, John James Audubon had witnessed a flock that took three days to pass overhead, obscuring the sun all the while. We did not intend to exterminate the passenger pigeon, but we did. It was not a governmental policy, but rather the collective actions of millions of individuals, each following his own interests, that doomed the bird. The pattern that underlies this behavior has been understood for over 180 years, but we seem not to have learned the lesson completely, and our schools rarely teach it.

The Tragedy of the Commons

In 1832, just 56 years after Adam Smith's influential book, *The Wealth of Nations*,[2] English political economist William Forster Lloyd wondered why commonly held pastures routinely get degraded. Assuming that people are guided by self-interest, he reasoned that when the carrying capacity of a common area is reached, a herdsman might ask himself, "Should I add another animal to my herd?" His gain for doing so would be all his immediately, but the loss incurred by degrading the pasture would be shared among all the herdsmen, and delayed too, so he would probably choose to add another animal to his herd whenever he could. In the long term, the common property would be unable to feed *any* animals, and *everyone* would be hurt. Even when the herdsmen understood the long-run consequences of their actions, they still needed some coercive means of putting everyone's common good ahead of their personal gain. Hence the often necessary, but hated, role of regulations with teeth.

"If men were angels, no government would be necessary."
—James Madison, 1788

Eliminating the passenger pigeon surely was an error, but we learned from such episodes that hunting regulations sustain healthy game-animal populations, and today hunting and fishing regulations operate well to preserve our

---

1. Wilson, p. 121
2. Smith

common heritage of wild foods. Since caveman days our species has learned through trial and error, but, beginning with the 20th Century, we have slipped into a different era—a time when the consequences of errors can be permanent. We cannot redo the passenger-pigeon experiment. It might have been a relatively good thing that Harry Truman used nuclear weapons when we had only two, rather than waiting until we had 50,000 and then seeing whether global nuclear war really does wipe out all life on Earth. Currently we are experimenting to find out what releasing genetically modified organisms (GMOs) into the environment will do to our food base and health. It seems essential to move beyond such dangerous trial-and-error strategies.

Herders did not intend to destroy the common pasturage, but they did. We humans did not intend to eliminate any innocent species, but through repeated application of the tragedy of the commons, we have collectively exterminated in just 40 years the golden toad, the Zanzibar leopard, the Po'ouli bird, the Madeiran Large White Moth, the Tecopa Pupfish, the Pyrenean Ibex, the West African Black Rhinoceros, the Javan Tiger, Spix's Macaw, the Round Island Burrowing Boa, and the Dutch Alcon Blue Butterfly;[1] and these are only the larger, more visible species—each a potentially essential strand in the web of life, whose snapping surely affected those co-dependent with them.

There are many smaller strands in this web of life that we mindlessly attack on a daily basis—insects and bacteria. We take the short-term view of ridding our environment of the pesky critters rather than considering the consequences of actually being successful at that. We choose to use anti-bacterial products that kill *all* bacteria, even those that are beneficial to healthy living. Coexistence is the key. These species also want to survive, and, when threatened, they can multiply faster than we can invent new methods of control.

Consider the deadly cholera bacteria that live in dirty water. When the water is cleaned up, the cholera epidemic fades, but the cholera bacteria are *still* in the water, just in low quantities that don't sicken us. We suspect that in dirty water, the cholera bacteria are *also* fighting for survival, which keeps them desperately multiplying, but when the water is clean, they are content to live in harmless balance with everything else in the water.

Example of Mosquitoes in the Web of Life

Let's look at a small, seemingly insignificant insect that periodically shows up in the news—the mosquito—and our potential codependency with it. When one lands on your arm, it may seem to be in your best interest to swat it,

---

1. http://tinyurl.com/extinction-list

as you might contract West Nile Virus, which can be nasty. If killing one mosquito is good, then eliminating more mosquitoes should be better, and exterminating all mosquitoes might be really good; but not so fast.

Since the publication of Rachel Carson's *Silent Spring* in 1962, the world has become increasingly aware of the devastating effects that pesticides can have on populations of birds. The outcry over DDT led to its being banned in 1972, but many other chemicals have arisen in its place, and bird populations continue to decline, due not only to pesticide use, but also to habitat loss, climate change, mercury pollution, monoculture agriculture, feral cats, invasive species, and removal of hedgerows. The fewer the birds, the more the mosquitoes flourish, and, when human health is threatened, the first response is often to reach for the chemical sprays.

During 2012, about 5400 cases of West Nile Virus occurred in the US, mostly in Texas and the Midwest, killing about 250. About 20% of those bitten became ill with flu-like symptoms lasting for weeks, and about 1% developed severe infections that can cause life-threatening nervous-system complications like meningitis or encephalitis. No one likes to be bitten or get sick, so we kill mosquitoes, unwittingly following the tragedy of the commons. We serve our short-term best interests to the detriment of long-term survival.

Controlling West Nile Virus by spraying insecticides is probably a poor long-term choice, just as DDT was in the '50s. Spraying mosquitoes is expensive, nonselective, and must be kept up indefinitely. Eventually, resistant mosquito strains will evolve, just as the deadly Carbapenem-Resistant Enterobacteriaceae (CRE),[1] has now evolved to resist *all* antibiotics. This bacterium kills half of those it infects and is present in 4% of American hospitals.

To control West Nile Virus, Dallas sprayed Permethrin, which kills honey bees, fish, and aquatic invertebrates. Honey bees produce about 30% of our food supply (see page 125), and aquatic invertebrates are at the root of a food chain that supports healthy rivers and streams, destruction of which can have dire long-term effects. Mosquitoes are, whether we like it or not, a key part of the web of life.

Joanne Lauck reports that over $150 million is spent each year on mosquito control through the use of pesticides that also harm mosquitoes' natural predators and other non-target species. Thousands of acres of swamps are drained each year, destroying other species that depend on mosquitoes for sustenance. Mosquito researcher Lewis Nielsen has found 30 species of flowering plants on mosquito bodies, so we know they are very important pollinators of

---

1. http://tinyurl.com/NightmareBacteria

wildflowers.[1] Each plant species supports 10 to 30 animal species, any one of which could be one we depend on as well. When we kill mosquito populations, we are breaking random strands in the web of life that supports us, which can, at some inopportune moment, be one strand too many. Then it will be game over, with no replay.

"No man is an island," said John Donne. We are in this together, all people, all plants, all animals, including all other insects, who deserve a place where they can play their role on the Earth stage. Remember, insects can live without us; we cannot live without them.

What Can We Do?

- We can use pro-active mosquito control, which is effective, free, and harmless to honey bees and streams. Place a light-colored bowl of water outside your door and let it stagnate. After feeding, female mosquitoes will lay hundreds of eggs there, which hatch into larvae, or wigglers, in two days. Adults will try to emerge after a week, and can live up to two months, biting and spreading disease, so monitor your bowl regularly and empty it and refill it each week after the wigglers appear, but before adults emerge, which breaks the reproduction chain. The wigglers die once they are out of water. The mosquito danger in your area will soon be much reduced.

- Donate, if you can, to the Nature Conservancy,[2] or a similar organization that preserves natural wetlands where Nature can live in peace. In these areas all of nature can thrive in balance.

Entomologists now agree that if all insects would suddenly disappear,
humans would not be able to survive
in new conditions longer than 10 years.
This is why entomologists should carefully use pest-control methods.
—Jean Henri Fabre, entomologist 1823-1915

ASSUMPTIONS ABOUT OUR FOOD

We have Food and Health side by side, because the two are inseparable. We are what we eat—literally. We have always assumed that when we go to the grocery store, there will be fresh, safe food on the shelves, but food that looks safe can be a future health issue in disguise, as we are finding out today.

1. Lauck
2. http://my.nature.org/donate

The EPA reports that between 1988 and 2007 American pesticide use increased by 56%. Over the same period, asthma, autism, learning disabilities, birth defects, reproductive dysfunction, diabetes, Parkinson's, Altzheimer's and several types of cancers have all increased and are linked to pesticide exposure. For example, 41 studies link pesticides to asthma, which has skyrocketed since the mid-1980s to epidemic levels, and 260 studies link pesticides to various forms of cancer, according to Beyond Pesticides, which maintains the Pesticide-Induced Diseases Database.[1] There are many more.

High-fructose corn syrup (HFCS) was introduced 40 years ago and by 1984, it was in most sodas. Today it comprises almost half of our sugar intake. Dr. Mark Hyman, a board-certified family medicine physician, explains that HFCS is an industrial food product extracted from corn stalks that is not processed the same way in the body. Regular cane sugar (sucrose) is made of two-sugar molecules bound tightly together in pairs. The enzymes in our digestive tract break down these molecules, which are then absorbed into the body. HFCS also consists of the same two molecules, but they are unbound and require no digestion. Consequently, they get absorbed rapidly into our bloodstream. The fructose heads straight to the liver and begins *lipogenesis*—the production of fats and cholesterol, which is the cause, he believes, of 70 million Americans now suffering from "fatty liver." When glucose is rapidly absorbed, it spikes our insulin, which is our body's fat-storage hormone. Both reactions lead to metabolic disturbances that increase appetite, weight gain, diabetes, heart disease, cancer, dementia and other chronic diseases plaguing us today.[2]

Dr. Hyman also points out that the reason that HFCS is used in such great quantities for industrial food production is because it is sweeter and cheaper than products made from cane sugar, but it is only cheaper because of government farm-bill corn subsidies that we tax payers ultimately pay. In other words, the price of corn is not a "true price." (See page 134.) We pay in hidden taxes to lower the price on a product that probably is not in our best health interests.

GMOs are plants with laboratory-altered DNA that became commercially available in 1994. Before their introduction, everyone was assured that they were safe. No long-term studies were completed on their safety until 2012. Gilles-Eric Seralini of the University of Caen conducted a chronic toxicity study, which showed the effects of eating GMOs over a rat's lifetime. The rats were fed NK603, Monsanto's variety of GM corn, which is the same corn found in many breakfast cereals, corn tortillas and corn chips. Some of their findings: 50% of males and 70% of females died prematurely; rats fed GM

---

1. http://www.beyondpesticides.org
2. http://tinyurl.com/DrHymanHFCSdiseases

corn and traces of Roundup suffered severe liver and kidney damage; rats that drank trace amounts of Roundup at levels *legally* allowed in the water supply had a 200% to 300% increase in large tumors. The study also found that "rats exposed to even the smallest amounts developed mammary tumors...as early as four months in males, and seven months in females."[1] Seralini's study has been disputed by experts in France, but his paper was published in the peer-reviewed journal, *Food and Chemical Toxicology*. In support of Seralini, other scientists have set up a website to counter all challenges to the study.[2]

In the late 1990s, Monsanto introduced into our food system its genetically modified Bt corn, which includes a gene from a soil bacterium called *Bacillus thuringiensis* (Bt), which produces the Bt toxin. Bt is a pesticide that breaks open the stomach of insects and kills them. The goal was fewer pests in the corn fields. However, Bt has now led to Bt-resistant insects, which should have been no surprise, since this is what life does—it adapts in order to live. Beyond resistant insects, stories are propagating about the negative effects Bt corn is having on human health. A study done in 2012 at Quebec's Sherbrooke University Hospital[3] found Bt toxin in the blood of 93% of pregnant women tested, in 80% of their babies' umbilical blood, and in the blood of 67% of non-pregnant women. The study speculates that the Bt toxin probably came from normal, Canadian middle-class diets of processed foods and drinks containing HFCS, which almost certainly contains Bt. This toxin can also be absorbed into your body by eating meat from animals who were fed Bt corn, which is what most animal-feeding operations use.

Currently about 95% of soybean and cotton acreage, and over 85% of corn acreage is now planted in Roundup-resistant GM varieties. A 2012 peer-reviewed study by Washington State University research professor Charles Benbrook found that the use of genetically engineered Roundup-resistant crops since 1999 has caused a 40% *annual* increase in the demand for herbicides to control the spread of Roundup-resistant "superweeds."[4] The pattern is the same—overuse leads to Mother Nature's counterbalancing reaction. Did we think she wouldn't notice this time?

The jury is still out on other GMO experiments, such as the one by AquaBounty Technologies of Boston which has inserted into the genome of an Atlantic salmon DNA from another salmon species and an eel-like fish, forcing the genetically engineered (GE) salmon produce growth hormones year round

1. http://tinyurl.com/RoundupTumors
2. http://gmoseralini.org
3. http://tinyurl.com/GMFoodToxins
4. http://tinyurl.com/GMOsAndSuperWeeds

rather than the normal three months a year.[1] These salmon are ready for market in 18 months instead of 30 and are a much larger size.

As if that were not enough, the assumption that our food crops will be automatically pollinated is now uncertain. Bees produce about a third of all human food, and their numbers are dwindling sharply around the world. "It's the worst year I've ever seen, really, in about 30 years, as bee losses go," said Joe Traynor, a widely respected bee broker in Bakersfield, Calif., a primary almond-growing area.[2] Dr. Gordon Wardell, Paramount Farming Company bee biologist, said 1.6 million bee hives are needed to pollinate California's almond crops, but only 0.4 million colonies remain.[3] Radio-frequency radiation from cell-phone towers is a major suspect (see page 133) as are the new central-nervous-system neo-nicotinoid pesticides, which are now banned in Europe.[4] China has lost many of its pollinators through over-using pesticides and over-harvesting honey. Workers in Sichuan Province now pollinate pear and apple trees by hand,[5] which is clearly uneconomical in the US. While we can live solely on wind-pollinated grains, life is much more enjoyable with the rich variety in food that honey bees enable.

Table 1. Foods That Depend Upon Honey Bees	
Alfalfa	Grapes
Allspice	Grapefruits
Almonds	Kiwifruits
Anise	Macadamia Nuts
Apples	Mangos
Apricots	Melons
Avocados	Nutmeg
Bananas	Papayas
Blackberries	Peaches
Blueberries	Pear
Cardamom	Peppermint
Cashews	Pumpkins
Cherries	Raspberry
Chocolate	Sesame
Coconut	Strawberries
Coffee	Sugarcane
Coriander	Tea Plants
Cranberries	Tequila (Agave)
Dairy Products (Alfalfa)	Tomatoes
Figs	Vanilla

1. http://tinyurl.com/FDAtoApproveGMOfish
2. http://tinyurl.com/FewerBeeHives
3. http://tinyurl.com/BeeHiveShortage
4. http://tinyurl.com/NeoNicsBanned
5. http://tinyurl.com/ChinaHandPollination

"It's easy to forget that we are as fragile as any other link in the ecosystem. It's easy to forget, because we feel like masters of our world."
—Esperanza Spalding, Musician and Activist

Another assumption we make is that our stores will always be fully stocked, but our food-distribution network is vulnerable to disruption by fuel shortages, communication failures, contamination, and economic volatility. During the summer of 2012, one could not turn on the TV news for more than a few minutes before seeing coverage of widespread drought, cracked ground, dry ponds, and massive infestations of insects. Crops withered, and cattle were being sold off.

Common sense suggests a causal relationship between the rise in consumption of unnatural foods and a similar rise in chronic illnesses and cancers. We would be well advised as a society to cultivate the widest possible variety of sustainable, heirloom food crops to enhance biodiversity, provide much low-skilled employment and help protect future populations. GMO crops are like land mines that have lain quietly for years before unexpectedly exploding and hurting innocents, which seems to be occurring. This knowledge may seem bleak and discouraging, but many good shifts are occurring as well—the biggest one being the increase in the number of small farms. (See more encouraging news in "The Certainty of Hope," on page 137.)

What can we do?

- We can buy food at our local farmers' markets, and urge supermarkets to buy local produce; many are.

- We can grow more of our own food, or join a local Community Supported Agricultural (CSA) program, which supports local farmers.

- We can join a seed library, where people bring in organic seeds at the end of a season and check out new ones in the spring.[1]

- We can buy and use local honey, for our health and to support our local beekeepers, so bees can keep doing their job.

- We can keep our stockpiled food rotating and fresh so we can withstand any short-term shortages.

- We can try to live in balance with the insects, for many of them are essential to our food supply.

- We can avoid pesticide use and encourage others to do the same.

---

1. http://seedlibraries.org

- We can make wise food choices and find out what foods contain GMOs, so we can decide whether or not to eat them.

- We can urge our elected officials to require that GMO foods be labeled, so making clear choices is easier.

ASSUMPTIONS ABOUT OUR HEALTH

A century ago many people in America died from infectious diseases like pneumonia and influenza. Medical science basically conquered such diseases and extended life expectancy for the first time in centuries, and we began to assume that we would all enjoy longer, healthier lives. However, as we marched merrily on toward longevity, chronic diseases such as heart disease, cancer, stroke and diabetes began to not only kill us, but to also plague us for decades while decreasing our quality of life. At the same time, our food changed from whole to processed foods with potentially harmful additives, dyes and GMOs.

Our annual sugar intake increased from 26 pounds per person 20 years ago to 135 pounds today, mainly due to all the hidden sugars we consume in sodas, sport drinks and processed foods. As we noted in the food section, this sugar intake shifted from ingesting only cane sugar to mainly HFCS. Along with this increase and shift to HFCS, it is understandable that the incidence of type-II diabetes has risen as well. Today approximately 186,000 American children and teenagers have diabetes, and an estimated 57 million people have pre-diabetes, putting them at high risk.[1] Unfortunately, this is not the only health issue that has increased.

One of the assumptions we've always made, which, sadly, is changing, is that our children will live longer than we do. In 2005, *The New York Times* reported the disturbing news that, for the first time in two centuries, "the current generation of children in America may have shorter life expectancies than their parents."[2] As of 2013, changes are being initiated to improve the diets and exercise habits of our children, but we still have a long way to go.

In September 2010, ABC News reported an appalling 30% increase in cancer among US children since 1990.[3] Between 1955 and 2009, our daily per-capita dye consumption increased from 11 mg to 60 mg, along with big increases in consumption of sugar, HFCS, chemical preservatives, and Bt-corn products.[4] Common sense suggests a causal connection.

---

1. http://tinyurl.com/Diabetes-Facts-Web-MD
2. http://tinyurl.com/ObesityKillingKids
3. http://tinyurl.com/YoungLobbiest.
4. http://tinyurl.com/CSPI-FoodDyes.

A new health issue is growing, called *leaky-gut syndrome,* in which the intestinal lining becomes more porous than it should be, allowing toxins, undigested food particles, and bacteria to enter the bloodstream. Dr. Craig Maxwell has concluded that this syndrome can arise from various sources, including a diet of refined flour and sugar, soda, food dyes, preservatives, and additives and artificial colors, but other contributing factors include the overuse of pain killers and antacids, excessive alcohol consumption, and tobacco smoking. The syndrome is hard to diagnose because it can express in so many different ways, such as autoimmune diseases, eczema, psoriasis, fatigue, joint pain, food allergies, arthritis, and learning difficulties.[1]

Dr. Bruce Ames of the Children's Hospital Oakland Research Institute explains how leaky-gut syndrome can come from consuming Bt-laden HFCS: The cells of our intestinal membrane are held together by "tight junctions" to keep food and bacteria inside. The high doses of unbounded, free fructose that exist in HFCS "have been proven to literally punch holes in the intestinal lining, allowing nasty by-products of toxic gut bacteria and partially digested food proteins to enter your blood stream." This leakage can "trigger the inflammation that we know is at the root of obesity, diabetes, cancer, heart disease, dementia and accelerated aging." This HFCS fructose should not be confused with naturally occurring fructose in fruit, which does not exhibit the same biological effects, but is digested naturally by the body.[2]

If food leaks out of the intestines and directly into the bloodstream, it does not get processed naturally, and the body does not recognize it as food. It triggers an allergic reaction. Common sense suggests a causal connection between the 70% of American food that now contains Bt-laden HFCS and the 20% increase in peanut allergies and 50% increase in overall children's food allergies since 1997.[3] This rise in allergies mirrors the pattern of increase in the four most commonly planted GMO crops—corn, soy beans, canola, and cotton.

Allergies can also derive from too much cleanliness, believe it or not. Allergies increase with per-capita income, and German studies found that farm children who worked with animals had fewer allergies than their city counterparts. Our immune systems need regular exercise, or they become vulnerable.

Dr. Don Huber is an expert in the toxicity of GE foods. He has taught plant pathology, soil microbiology, and micro-ecological interactions in plant diseases at Purdue University for 35 years. He relates how agriculture is part of the *web of life* (see page 118). in that it is "a complete 'system' based on inter-

1. http://tinyurl.com/DrMaxwellLeakyGutSyndrome
2. http://tinyurl.com/GMratTumors
3. http://tinyurl.com/RiseInFoodAllergies

related factors, and in order to maintain ecological balance and health, you must understand how that system works as a whole."[1] Like all feedback systems, once you change one part of the system, you change the interaction of all other parts of it, because the web of life works together as a unit.

Monsanto created GE food crops with their patented Roundup Ready corn, cotton, soybean and sugar beets, which were engineered to survive normally lethal doses of *glyphosate*, Roundup's active ingredient. The theory was that by making plants resistant to the herbicide, farmers could increase their yield by suppressing weed growth, but as we mentioned, this is backfiring with the growth of superweeds.[2] The web of life was not honored.

Huber concludes that GE food crops contribute to many of today's health issues because "herbicides are chelators that form a barrier around specific nutrients, preventing whatever life form is seeking to utilize that element from utilizing it properly." This process not only applies to plants and soil microbes, but to animals and humans as well.

As Dr. Huber said, "*When future historians come to write about our era, they are not going to write about the tons of chemicals we did or didn't apply. When it comes to glyphosate, they are going to write about our willingness to sacrifice our children and to jeopardize our very existence by risking the sustainability of our agriculture; all based upon failed promises and flawed science. The only benefit is that it affects the bottom-line of a few companies. There's no nutritional value.*"[3]

And if it isn't bad enough that diseases in our children are increasing, after the 2008 financial and economic crisis, there was also a dramatic increase in American hunger, which is persisting. In 2010, 17.2 million households (approximately one in seven), were "food insecure." This is a new term, which means that at times during the year, the household food intake was reduced and normal eating patterns were disrupted because of lack of money and other food resources. This is the highest number ever recorded in the US, supposedly the richest country in the world.[4]

What can we do?

There are always choices. We can keep eating as we have been and hope for the best, or we can take personal responsibility and change our diets little by little to more whole foods, like those our ancestors ate for millennia before us. As good as our medical doctors are at putting us back together physically after

---

1. http://tinyurl.com/HuberGEtoxicity
2. http://tinyurl.com/RoundupTolerantSuperWeeds
3. http://tinyurl.com/NoNutritionalValue
4. http://tinyurl.com/AmericanHunger

injuries—brilliantly at times—they cannot perform miracles to quickly fix us after our bodies have consumed poor food and beverages for decades. The body has miraculous healing abilities. If we nourish it with the food it is meant to have, it will respond. If we exercise, it will get strong. If we reduce our drug and alcohol intake, our livers will heal. And, we can just quit smoking, or at least cut down. Daily choices have long-term effects.

And the good news is that many of the chronic health issues that plague people today—heart disease, diabetes, obesity, lung disease, and high blood pressure—can be significantly improved through a balanced diet of whole, non-processed foods (preferably organic) containing vegetables, fruits, whole grains and small amounts of meat. Our bodies were meant to eat non-chemicalized food, with sugar as a rare treat, as it once was.

Additionally for health:

- We are not machines, and we know our bodies—or we should, so if your doctor doesn't really listen to you, find another.

- We can build up our immune systems; see page 71.

- We can reduce our use of antibacterial products and allow the good bacteria to naturally counterbalance the bad.

- We can take antibiotics only when really needed. Remember they don't affect viruses, which are what most colds and flus are.

- Volunteer at food banks or other organizations that pack up food for children to take home over the weekend.

ASSUMPTIONS ABOUT OUR MEDICAL INSTITUTIONS

We Americans assume that we have the best medical care in the world, but it seems to be steadily declining. Costs are high, many can't afford medical insurance or care, leading to 44 million uninsured, and 30 million under-insured in the US. Doctors and nurses are overworked, and the shortage is increasing.

We assume that when we go to the hospital we'll come out healthy, and, mostly, we do. However, we often ignore the fact that one of the top-ten categories of causes of death is always *iatrogenic*, meaning that someone died as a direct result of a doctor's treatment, whether via misdiagnosis or from adverse reactions to drugs that were prescribed. The reported cause of death is usually listed as being the final factor, rather than the medical error that caused it. In 2010, HealthGrades, a health care quality company,[1] in a study of 37 million patient records, reported that an average of 195,000 Americans died due to

---

1. http://tinyurl.com/MedicalErrorDeaths

potentially preventable, in-hospital medical errors, which is 3,750 people a *week* dying from medical errors.

What Can We Do?

Tips to make you safer during hospital visits:

- If you must enter the hospital for a planned surgical visit, make sure you confirm your name, allergies and what body part is in need of repair, if they don't. Most do.

- Plan ahead and trade with a friend to be advocates for each other so if you have an emergency visit to the hospital, this person can monitor your treatments and medications.

- Be extra alert during shift changes, which is when information often falls through the cracks, when a staffer who is leaving fails to convey all the information needed to the one coming on duty.

- Stay informed: know what is on your chart and don't be afraid to ask what meds you are on and what they are for.

TIP
TO SAVE MONEY, BEFORE ANY HOSPITAL PROCEDURE, NEGOTIATE THE
PRICE OF THE PROCEDURE THROUGH HEALTHCAREBLUEBOOK.COM
AND FIND OUT WHAT MEDICARE AND MEDICAID PAY AT CMS.GOV

ASSUMPTIONS ABOUT OUR WATER

We are still blessed with water when we turn on the tap, but it doesn't always taste good, unless you happen to still have a well with some minerals and life to it. Municipal water is often an unpleasant chemical soup of chlorine and pharmaceuticals that have been excreted or dumped upstream. We assume in our myopia that flushing leftover drugs down the toilet would make them disappear—out of sight, out of mind—not realizing that in the long-term, they don't. Current water-treatment technology cannot remove them. Americans consume 30 gallons of bottled water annually, only to find PBA leaching into the water from the plastic, mimicking sex hormones, and bringing on early puberty in girls. Alternatively, we can drink water containing recycled pharmaceuticals. It's not a pleasant choice.

Water is the next oil, in the sense that its scarcity is already causing major conflicts around the world. There is no alternative to it. Each North American uses over 1860 cubic meters of it per year.

While more than 70% of our Earth's surface is covered by water, over 97% of it is salty, leaving less than 3% as fresh water, nearly 70% of which is frozen in icecaps. Most of the rest is soil moisture or lies in inaccessible aquifers deep underground. Less than 1% of the world's fresh water (~0.007% of all water on Earth) is available for direct human use. This water is found in lakes, rivers, reservoirs and underground sources shallow enough to be tapped affordably. This small portion is regularly renewed by rain and snowfall, and is therefore available on a sustainable basis, but it is not growing, as is world population and its associated water demand, so a challenge lies ahead.

According to the World Water Assessment Program, 2 million tons of human waste are dumped daily in waterways. In developing countries, 70% of industrial wastes are also dumped, untreated, into surface waters. Half of all wetlands, incubators for much of the world's wildlife, have been lost since 1900, which has led to species loss and lower fish inventories.

Long-term solutions to water-supply issues are entangled with energy issues. A typical fracking well may use up to 4 million gallons of water and contaminate much of the surrounding ground water. The best thing we can do for our water sources is not to pollute them in the first place. Another long-term source of potable water is to use abundant solar energy to desalinate sea-water. The higher price of such water may be the long-term "true price" of water, to which we will need to get accustomed. (See page 134.)

What can we do?

- We can use water wisely, all the time, use less fossil and more renewable energy to reduce the demand for fracking, which destroys our water sources.

- We can help prevent water pollution whenever we can.

- We can safely dispose of leftover drugs: If no disposal instructions are on the label and no take-back program is available, mix the pills with an undesirable substance, like old coffee grounds or kitty litter so children, pets, or folks browsing through your trash won't take them. Put them in a sealable bag, can, or other container to prevent leakage,[1] and then put it in the trash. This will help keep them out of the water system.

- We can urge leaders to preserve natural waterways and wetlands.

- We can buy filters for our sinks and showers, or household filters that clean up all water entering the home.

- We can use glass to avoid PBA leaching. (See also page 43.)

---

1. http://tinyurl.com/DisposeOfMeds

Assumptions about our Technology

We have been enjoying the increase in our technological conveniences since the '50s, because they seem to make life better and better. European scientists, however, present growing evidence that RF (radio frequency) radiation from cell towers may have severe long-term health effects on humans.[1]

We assume that it is safe to live in an RF soup millions of times more intense than it was just 30 years ago. We assume that our well-being is unaffected by the unseen, but intense, bombardment we get every day from electromagnetic frequency (EMF) radiation from TV, radio, and cell phones.

To the naked eye, our planet appears to be unaffected, but the cellular level is experiencing the biggest change that life on Earth has ever endured, the effects of which we are just beginning to see and feel. Many people are developing cancers that are probably directly linked to this radiation, while most cancer victims have no idea what caused their illness.

These same European scientists have also discovered that RF radiation reduces the amount of melatonin our bodies produce at night, because our pineal gland mistakes RF radiation for light. Melatonin not only helps us sleep, but it is also a major antioxidant that sweeps up free radicals that are naturally created in our bodies by sunlight, radiation, chemicals, pollution, fumes, stress, exercise, and even the very act of metabolism and cellular respiration. According to the research, without regular production of melatonin, free radicals build up, and many diseases can result.

What can we do?

- We can power down wireless devices at night. We can't block incoming signals, but we don't have to contribute to the problem. We can replace Wi-Fi with cables, we know, not ideal!

- We can take melatonin before sleeping.

- We can eat foods that are naturally antioxidizing, like garlic (see page 73) and grape seeds (see page 75, and a good variety of whole grains, fruits and vegetables, plus take supplements such as Vitamins A, C and E, and beta-carotene.

Assumptions about our Economy

We always assumed that the free market economy efficiently balances supply and demand, that it encourages and makes best use of individual entrepreneur-

---

1. http://tinyurl.com/ResonanceRFdocumentary 90-minute video

ial abilities, and that it lets consumers choose how to earn and spend their income. But we cannot assume that what consumers want—sugar, fat, salt, *e.g.*,—is in their best long-term interests, because they do not always know the long-term consequence of their choices. Ideally, to be most effective, the free market needs full, free and instantaneous availability of all relevant information to all buyers and sellers, but that happens only in theory.

True Prices

In Adam Smith's day, if a cobbler on one side of the road made cheaper shoes by polluting the public fish pond and killing the fish, people would notice and would not buy his shoes just because they were cheaper. His prices were not "true" prices, because they did not reflect his true cost of production. People could see who was making the shoes and how. If they valued fresh fish in their diet, they would buy the shoes from the more expensive cobbler, who protected the fish pond. He offered "true" prices, *i.e.*, the prices that given goods or services must be sold at to protect priceless qualities like safety, human dignity, species diversity, and clean air, water, and land. True prices work best on a local scale, where one can see how things are done, and by whom.

Born with the new American nation, Adam Smith's influential 1776 book, *The Wealth of Nations*, claimed that some godlike Invisible Hand guides the free market to benefit all the citizens. All that was necessary was to let the market flow, unencumbered by regulations or other impediments. The business community championed the idea, and Adam Smith has been cited ever since. When people could see how products were made on a small scale in a village, the Invisible Hand worked well, but things have changed.

Extrapolating from a village to a planet is difficult. When consumers can no longer see the production process, the Invisible Hand goes blind, and it often hurts the common interest rather than serving it. For example, a consumer who sees two nearly identical competing products in a supermarket that seem to differ only in price, may buy the cheaper one. She cannot see that its lower price came from polluted rivers, or child labor, or a thousand other abuses that she would not support if she knew how the product was being made. The lowest price is usually not a "true" price. When we are not given full information and true prices, our choices can hurt the common good. Common sense suggests full disclosure of all information about goods and services.

In the 237 years since *The Wealth of Nations*, many people have lost confidence, not only in the Invisible Hand, but also in the ability of government to correct the situation. Self-serving lobbyists outnumber legislators in Washington, D.C. by 23 to 1. Ultimately, though, we consumers can move the market to respond to what we want.

TIP

YOU VOTE WITH YOUR PURCHASES, SO BUY WISELY.

Adam Smith's free market is not broken, but it is blind. One thing we can do is to return to a smaller scale when it makes sense to do so. We are seeing this in the "back to local" food movement everywhere.

We always assumed that our houses were an investment whose value would always increase, but a new reality hit us in the face when Wall Street began making opaque financial transactions that fooled millions into thinking they were investing, when, in fact, they were being taken for fools. The housing collapse and Great Recession followed, reducing the median net worth of US households by 47% between 2007 and 2010, reaching its lowest inflation-adjusted level since 1969.[1] We assumed that we would be able to find good-paying jobs, which is becoming more difficult, especially for recent college graduates who collectively hold over a trillion dollars in college-loan debt and many of whom have no choice but to live with their parents.

We always assumed banks would take care of our money. Times have changed. On April 29, 2013, the largest lender in Cyprus, the Bank of Cyprus, took care of itself first in what is now called a "bail-in." Reuters reported that the bank "had converted 37.5% of deposits exceeding 100,000 euros into 'class A' shares, with an additional 22.5% held as a buffer for possible conversion in the future. Another 30% would be temporarily frozen and held as deposits."[2] In other words, large depositors' cash accounts suddenly became market shares in a troubled corporation. Legendary trader Jim Sinclair wrote, "The message from Cyprus, which has also been written in various white papers and signed by central banks, the FDIC, Bank of England, and the BIS, is to *get out of the system.*" We are *not* financial advisors, so we cannot help you interpret his advice, but knowledge removes blinders and makes us more prepared for unexpected events, and this swift move by the Bank of Cyprus was definitely that.

We know that the stock market can be swayed by rumors and the public mood. On May 6, 2010, a mutual fund made an unusually large sell, and the Dow-Jones Industrial Average dropped 1000 points, only to recover within 20 minutes. On April 23, 2013, another "flash crash" occurred on Wall Street when a hacker penetrated the APTwitter Account. The hoaxer tweeted that explosions at the White House had injured President Obama, and within *seconds* the stock market crashed almost 150 points because the computers that drive it are programmed to sell on negative words in popular tweets (see

---

1. http://tinyurl.com/MedianWealthPlummets
2. http://tinyurl.com/CyprusFlushed

page 105). While the market index recovered within five minutes, some $200 billion had changed hands.

These mini-crashes would probably not have happened had humans been at the wheel, because they would have used *common sense*. With instant communication around the world and hackers attacking everywhere, we live in a new and unpredictable world. If hackers collapsed the market once, we can expect them to do so again, at their convenience. Again, forewarned is forearmed.

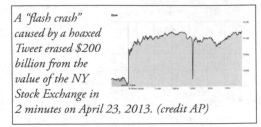

A "flash crash" caused by a hoaxed Tweet erased $200 billion from the value of the NY Stock Exchange in 2 minutes on April 23, 2013. (credit AP)

What can we do?

- We can stop assuming that housing prices will always rise, and purchase a house because we *can* afford it and *like* it.

- We can have patience—houses are still a solid investment. Already we're seeing many previously underwater homeowners emerging into daylight again.

- We can invest in companies in which we trust and believe.

- We can invest in mutual funds that invest our money in ways that support our values, rather than just chasing high returns.

- We can buy products that we know are made by people under good working conditions.

- We can be aware of how changes in the financial world may hurt us, and then make compensating changes.

Certainty

We have discussed uncertainties arising from cosmic events, nuclear war, breaks in the web of life, food, health, our medical system, water, technology, and our economy. There is so much uncertainty, but there is much good news, too. Everywhere, people are waking up and creating a better future. People demand safe food, for example, and even giant Walmart responds by stocking organic food. That is encouraging.

We hold the future in our hands, and that is hopeful.

Of that much we are certain.

16

The Certainty of Hope

EVERYTHING YOU NEED TO KNOW,
YOU LEARNED FROM NOAH'S ARK...
CELEBRATE THE RETURN OF THE DOVE.

One of the strengths of the American economic system has always been its responsiveness to change. Now our economic system is responding to the challenges of the day, and good things are happening.

William Greider[1] reports very good news from the world of American business. Small businesses have always been at the forefront of change, and they see the handwriting on the wall that says that long-term survival is impossible without sustainably created products. So the American Sustainable Business Council,[2] whose 160,000 business members promote "public policies that ensure a vibrant, just, and sustainable economy," is putting a business face on the need to find solutions to the issues before us. This organization transcends political affiliations and supports common sense.

Josh Knauer, president and CEO of the Pittsburgh software company Rhiza, suggests that sustainability is a good way to proceed: "I deeply believe in building resilient communities. This is what happens in ecosystems. A healthy ecosystem is resilient—it can withstand fire; it can withstand drought; basically, it can withstand anything you throw at it. When businesses are responsible to our communities, you build more resilient, thriving communities."

Such small businesses support the *triple*-bottom-line, essential objectives of *people, profit, and planet.* Corporations with better records on social behavior do better on returns and stock prices, so they anticipate wide funding support through the markets. Ally LaTourelle is vice-president of BioAmber, a company that produces biodegradable alternatives to replace toxic petrochemicals that are commonly used in many products. She is confident that the megacorporations will lose their fight against sustainability, because "these changes are really inevitable.... Stalling the inevitable is the most the industry can do."

She believes that small-business people can change things. "To me, sustainable business is not only about injecting the concept of the *public commons*

---

1. http://tinyurl.com/NewBusinessLeft
2. http://asbcouncil.org/

back into the marketplace, which is critical to our economic survival and social fabric," she says... "*It's also just plain common sense.*"

In May, 2013, several big clothing manufacturers signed on to a legally binding plan to improve safety conditions where cheap clothing is made, after a horrendous building collapse in Bangladesh[1] killed 1,127 workers April 24, 2013. This horrible tragedy was a "wake-up call" for the businesses involved, and hopefully, for all of us who love a bargain, but who now realize the *true costs* (see page 134) of low prices.

Here is more good news from inspiring, creative people, leading us forward into new ways of thinking and living.

Consider the farmers' markets that have grown from 1,755 in 1994 to 7,865 in 2012, including a 9.6% increase from 2011 to 2012 alone. In our small N.C. county, in addition to several farmer's markets, some forward-looking folks worked together to fix up an old school. They turned it into an "ag center"[2] that houses offices and a store, where local produce, food products, and crafts are sold, which not only provides us with fresh, local food, but also encourages more small farmers to return to old ways of nurturing and honoring their land, which honors the web of life.

Consider Detroit: after being devastated by the auto industry's decline, major job losses, and high crime, the city was almost gutted, but it is rising up out of the ashes to rebuild itself. Detroiters readjusted their long-held assumption that they could thrive *only* through the auto industry and that their town was dead. High-tech companies are now moving in and retraining people in new jobs. Detroit's Madison Building, built in 1917, now houses more than two dozen high-tech start-ups. Manufacturing jobs are being created to build watches and bicycles, and the US auto industry is rising up again with newly designed "green" cars for the future.

People who saw a silver lining in the empty lots replaced them with urban gardens, which now play a strong role in transforming the city. Schools and soup kitchens even raise produce in their own gardens, and a CSA (see page 126) set up by several Detroit farmers distributes city-grown produce.

To destroy the myth that Detroit has no neighborhood grocery stores, writer James Griffioen makes it clear that they do not have chain stores, but they do have locally owned and independent stores with fresh meats and produce, where the money earned recycles through the community. Detroit also has the Eastern Market Corporation (EMC), a huge Saturday market that

---

1. http://tinyurl.com/RealPriceOfCheapClothing
2. http://tinyurl.com/PolkCountyAgCenter

draws in 15,000 suburbanites every weekend. And in a not-so-random act of kindness, EMC makes fresh produce available to all Detroiters. Programs like "Double Up Food Bucks and "Michigan Mo' Bucks" are now in place to "provide families receiving food assistance benefits with the means to purchase more fresh fruits and vegetables at farmers' markets."[1]

Consider Greensburg, Kan., which was only two miles wide when a 1.5-mile-wide tornado destroyed the town in 2007. 90% of the population became instantly homeless. Within 12 hours, local officials decided to rebuild the town in a "green" way. After reassessing their "assumptions" about life, they cast aside old beliefs and politics and embraced low-impact reconstruction methods. The City Hall, which is now super-energy-efficient, was remade from reclaimed brick and wood; there is a solar and wind-powered art center; and the homes are being built as geodesic domes or other sustainable designs meant to withstand high winds. Perhaps Moore, Okla., and other towns devastated by the severe weather of late will follow their example.

Consider Orchard Gardens Elementary School, once one of the lowest performing K-8 schools in Massachusetts. Its designation as a "turnaround" school became a silver lining, as it gave them the flexibility they needed to change. Andrew Bott, their sixth principal in seven years, took the opportunity and replaced 80% of the previous staff, invested in recruiting experienced teachers, and extended the school day. He then shifted his entire $100,000 security budget into teaching the arts. Within three years the school was almost unrecognizable. Achievement essays and motivational posters now cover the halls. The school now has one of the fastest student-improvement rates in the state, and the students, once described as loud and unruly, are now thriving.[2] The children rose to the expectation around them.

Consider Sylvia Todd, the dynamic 11-year-old girl who produces with her dad a kids' science program on YouTube[3] with millions of hits. She is an energetic, motivating wonder in front of the camera. In April, 2013, she showed her water-color robot at the White House science fair, not only motivating other children, especially girls, but also adults to "learn something new."

Consider the children in an Australian primary school who decided to change the world using five minutes a day. They divided into groups, and each day one of the groups completed a project like collecting old mobile phones for proper disposal, planting vegetables in a school garden, turning off electricity

---

1. http://tinyurl.com/DetroitGroceries
2. http://tinyurl.com/OrchardGardensTurnAround
3. http://tinyurl.com/SlyviaScience

anywhere in the school that was not in use, recycling old books and toys via a free garage sale, and even sharing jokes just to lift spirits.

Consider fifth-grader Dalton Sherman, who spoke to 20,000 Dallas School District employees, stressing how belief in each other helps all of us rise to our highest level. He said he believed in himself, but without *their* belief, none of the 157,000 students could do it alone. Speaking to all the staff, he said, "*You* matter, because next week we're all showing up in *your* schools, and what we need from *you* is to believe that *we* can reach our highest potential."[1]

Consider the church movement to do a better job of "dominion" over God's Creation. The Methodist Green Church Association urges churches to save energy and water and to use safer cleaning and pest-control agents. The Madison Christian Community restored native prairie grass around their rural church, so instead of spending money to control their lawn with hazardous chemicals, now graceful prairie grass blows freely in the wind, as it did centuries ago. They also added solar power and cut their power usage by 40%.

Consider the Interfaith Climate and Energy Campaign, which urges churches to conserve, because most church buildings are old and inefficient. The philosophy of these forward-looking clergy is to encourage each of us to begin taking care of something manageable—like our corner of the world, which is a first start and does make a difference. The "4/1 Earth Mission" of the Green Justice Congregations of the United Church of Christ completed 50 Great Days of restoring the environment, during which time they planted 100,000 trees. They speak for all of us: "Our work of saving this sacred place, our planet, is far from done, and it must continue."

We all rise to the level of expectation—individually and societally—so let's all expect good things of ourselves and others and then rise to that higher level as a society. It is the least we can do for the as-yet unborn who await us in our not-yet-realized, but sustainable, future.

Sometimes life can look confusing and bleak, but with all the innovative changes going on, and with so many amazing children helping us to shift our old assumptions, we have *nothing to fear*. Nature always has faith in tomorrow's arrival. She knows that all her needs will be met, so let's expect the same.

May Nature and Everything We Hold Sacred guide us all through...

Listening, Observing and Learning...

And *Laughing Out Loud!*   LOL

---

1. http://tinyurl.com/DaltonSpeaks video

Summer Arrived

Summer arrived on a spider's web,
Mid-afternoon, just yesterday.
Like an old friend,
Asleep in the corner,
Forgotten under the shrouds of winter.

Summer arose,
Inhaling the remnants of a colder time,
Breathing warmth into Those Who Waited.

The little girl knew exactly what to do,
Crafting a perfect orb,
Not six inches wide,
Without classes,
Parents or siblings,
To teach her the intricacies of her task.

She had no news
To worry her about
Some distressing drop in insect populations,
No thoughts of scarcity,
No doubts of self-sufficiency.

But following some inner guidance,
She wove her trembling sail,
Which she hoisted on masts of twigs,
To carry herself bravely forth
Upon an unknown but supportive sea
On a journey across the Web of Life.

Brian L. Crissey

About the Authors

Brian L. Crissey, Ph.D.

Brian received his B.E.S in Operations Research and his Ph.D. in Computer Science from the Johns Hopkins University. He served as a computer specialist with the Joint Chiefs of Staff during the Vietnam Conflict and worked as a staff member on the Committee On Nuclear and Alternative Energy Systems for the National Academy of Sciences (NAS) in Washington, D.C. He co-authored *Models in the Policy Process* and, was synthesis staff officer for the NAS study *Energy in Transition, 1985-2010: Final Report of the Committee on Nuclear and Alternative Energy Systems.* Taking what he learned about energy choices and risks to Illinois, he became active in working against the proliferation of nuclear weapons and nuclear power plants. His research into their use and potentially devastating destruction led him to believe that we all need to be aware of our surroundings and know what to do if an unexpected disaster strikes.

He taught computer science and mathematics at the collegiate level for many years at Illinois State University, Linfield College, and North Greenville University. With his wife Pam he co-founded in 1991 what is now the Granite Publishing Group, which has published more than 70 titles, including the first edition of this book shortly after the 9/11 events.

Pamela Meyer Crissey, C.H.

Over the years, Pam found herself in crisis predicaments—a possible sudden evacuation while living on Cyprus, living within 40 miles of Three Mile Island and a year later living a similar distance from Mt. St. Helens when it erupted. These incidents cemented a need in her mind to be ready for the unexpected.

She is the President of the Granite Publishing Group, a diverse publishing company that she and Brian began in 1991. Before becoming a publisher, Pam worked for Apple Computer and Tektronix. She studied homeopathic healing in McMinnville, Ore., learned herbal healing at the School of Natural Healing in North Carolina and became a Chartered Herbalist through the Dominion Herbal College in Vancouver, B.C. She became an ordained minister in the Alliance of Divine Love in 2010.

Common Sense in Uncommon Times is their first co-authored publishing project. In their spare time they conduct educational and spiritual programs at the Crystal Creek Center in Western North Carolina.

Checklists

EVERYTHING YOU NEED TO KNOW, YOU LEARNED FROM NOAH'S ARK...
DON'T LISTEN TO CRITICS—
JUST GET ON WITH THE JOB THAT NEEDS TO BE DONE.

Emergency Telephone Numbers and Web Sites

- Center for Disease Control: 800-CDC-INFO www.cdc.gov
- Poison Control Center: 800-222-1222
- American Red Cross: www.redcross.org/find-your-local-chapter
- FBI: 202-324-3000 www.fbi.gov
- National Mental Health Association: 800-969-6642 www.mentalhealthamerica.net

Table 1. My Emergency Numbers

Who	Number

All of the tables in this section can be downloaded as PDFs at
http://granitepublishing.us/CommonSense

Table 2. First-aid Kit Add-ins

Item	Note
First Aid Kit	Purchase a quality kit
Carmex lip protection	for canker sores
Aspirin or similar	pain reliever
Anti-diarrhea medication	(see page 91)
Laxative	(see page 89)
Activated charcoal	(see page 93)
Honey, sugar and salt	(see page 78)
Mole Skin blister care	for *Go Pack*, hiking out unexpectedly
Antibacterial Salve	
Hydrocortisone	for stings (or see page 80)
Herbal or homeopathic remedies	according to your needs
Sunscreen	according to sun intensity and your sensitivity

Table 3. Special Medical Needs

Who	What

Understanding the Item Lists

The following item lists are organized in descending order of importance, although your specific situation may vary. The columns have the following meaning:

- Item: Description of the item
- I: Importance, from10=essential, to more optional
- Q: Check this when you have this item completed, or enter the quantity you have
- Need: Quantity recommended

Table 4. *Go Pack* Item List

Item	I	Q	Need
blanket, mylar space	10		1 item/person
4 in 1 LED Emergency Dynamo FM/AM Radio-flashlight, crank to charge	10		1 item/person
spare eyeglasses, contacts & solution	10		as needed
5-in-1 survival whistle	10		1 item/person
items, sacred	10		1 item/person
note pad, paper and pencil	10		1 set/person
Solar Charger for all portable devices	10		1 item/family
This Book	10		1 item/family
sanitary pads for bleeding	10		As needed
water	10		2 4 qts
Potable Aqua Water Treatment Tablets	10		4 tablets/pers/day
map, local topographical, with roads	10		1 item/person
paper, toilet	10		1 roll/person
waste bags	10		1 item/person
tool, multi-purpose, or Swiss Army knife	10		1 item as needed
underwear	10		1 item/person
medications, personal	10		1 item as needed
portable first-aid kit	10		1 item/person
box of waterproof matches, or Emergency Fire Starter	10		1 item/family

Table 4. *Go Pack* **Item List**

Item	I	Q	Need
Light My Fire TinderSticks	10		2 item/person
bandana or handkerchief	10		1 item/person
Natural Remedy Kit (page 70)	9		1 set/family
cord, nylon	9		50 feet/person
poncho, hooded	9		1 item/person
hat, sun	9		1 item/person
footwear, comfortable walking	9		1 pair/person
sunscreen	9		1 item/family
flannel shirt	9		item/person
shovel, small utility	9		1 item/family
bag, large trash	8		1 bag/person
eyeglass repair kit	8		1 kit as needed
lip protection	8		1 item/person
plastic tubing, wrapped with duct tape	8		6 ft./person
socks, wool	8		1 pair/person
insect repellent	8		1 item/person
mirror, signaling, or an old CD	8		1 item/person
sheeting, plastic, 1 mil, 6' sq.	8		1 item/person
glasses, sun	8		1 item/person
money, small bills and change	8		As needed
batteries, extra, all types in use	8		2 item/person
long pants	8		1 pair/person
food, dried and/or MREs (see page 57)	8		3-4 meals/person
mask, dust, N95 NIOSH-approved	8		2 items/person
goggles, swimming	8		1 item/person
compass (see also page 16.)	8		1 item/person
bulb, extra	7		1 item/person
cap, wool stocking	7		1 item/person
gloves, leather-palm warm work	7		1 pair/person
Hot Hands	7		as needed
tissue packages	7		1 package/person

Table 4. *Go Pack* **Item List**

Item	I	Q	Need
towelettes	7		1 pack/person
towel, small	7		1 item/person
mess kit	7		1 set/family
30-hour candle	6		1 item/person
lighter, childproof	5		1 item/person
blades, razor	5		as needed
sewing kit, with safety pins	5		1 set/family
long thermal underwear	5		as needed
waterproof pouch, to keep things dry	4		1 item/person
utensils, plastic eating	4		1 set/person
mosquito netting	4		1 item/person
wire, snare	4		1 feet/person
cap, shower, for rain hat	3		1 item/person
tape, survey, to mark trails	3		1 item/person
cards, playing	3		1 deck/family
portable stove and fuel tablets	3		as needed

Vehicle Box Item List

Item	I	Q	Need
	10		1 item/vehicle
...l highway (phones fail)	10		1 item/vehicle
...nking and washing	10		6 qts/person
...i-purpose	10		1 item as needed
jack, car and tire iron	10		1 set/vehicle
jumper cables	10		1 item/vehicle
box of waterproof matches, or lighter	9		1 item/person
Light My Fire TinderSticks	9		2 item/person
pencil and paper	9		1 item/family
fire extinguisher, A-B-C type	9		1 item/family
tools, automotive	9		1 set/vehicle
fuses	8		1 item/vehicle

Table 5. Vehicle Box Item List

Item	I	Q	Need
hose, short rubber, for siphon	8		1 item/person
batteries, extra, all types in use	8		2 items/person
blanket	8		1 item/person
oil, motor	8		1 quart/vehicle
poncho, hooded	8		1 item/person
bulb, extra	7		1 item/person
flare, signal	7		4 items/vehicle
hatchet	7		1 item/vehicle
bag, sealable plastic	5		1 item/vehicle
money	5		$10/person
transmission fluid	5		1 quart/vehicle
book, good reading	5		1 item as needed
rope, tow	5		50'/vehicle
steering fluid	4		1 bottle/vehicle

Table 6. Stash Item List (10 & above: Portable)

Item	I	Q	Need
duffle bag on wheels, to carry portables	10		1 item/family
can opener, manual	10		1 item/family
photos of loved ones	10		as needed
lighter, childproof	10		1 item/person
pencil and note pad	10		3 item/family
spare eyeglasses, contacts & solution	10		as needed
gloves, warm work	10		1 pair/person
items, sacred	10		as needed
sanitary pads for bleeding	10		as needed
water	10		4 qt/person/day

Table 6. Stash Item List (10 & above: Portable)

Item	I	Q	Need
Potable Aqua Water Treatment Tablets	10		4 tablets/pers/day
potable water filter	10		1 item/family
paper, toilet	10		1 roll/person
radio, battery-powered	10		1 item/family
wrench, shut-off	10		1 item/person
batteries, extra, all types in use	10		4 item/person
tool, multi-purpose	10		1 item/as needed
poncho, hooded	10		1 item/person
underwear	10		1 item/person
long pants	10		1 pair/person
footwear, comfortable durable walking	10		1 pair/person
knife, Swiss Army	10		as needed
medications, personal	10		as needed
Natural Remedy Kit	10		1 item/family
food, dried	10		10 item/person
stove, camping and fuel	10		1 item/family
deluxe first-aid kit	10		1 item/family
food, dried and/or MREs (see page 57)	10		12 meals/person
food, canned	10		as needed
winter coat	10		as needed
sleeping bags	10		1 item/person
two-person tube tent	10		as needed
box of waterproof matches, or lighter	9		1 item/person
utensils, plastic eating	9		1 set/person
bag, large trash	9		10 bag/person
cap, wool stocking	9		1 item/person
cord, nylon	9		50 feet/person
duct tape	9		1 roll/family
Light My Fire TinderSticks	9		2 item/person
hat, sun	9		1 item/person
money	9		as needed

Table 6. Stash Item List (10 & above: Portable)

Item	I	Q	Need
nylon rope	9		100 feet/family
book, good reading	9		as needed
bucket-lid toilet seat	9		1 item/family
footwear, light-weight	9		1 item/person
tarps	9		1 item/family
flannel shirt	9		1 item/person
water filter, non-electric	9		1 item/person
Aluminum foil	8		1 roll/family
blanket, mylar space	8		1 item/person
flashlight	8		1 item/person
Hot Hands	8		2 itcm/person
lip protection	8		1 item/person
papers, copies of important	8		1 set/family
sewing kit, with safety pins	8		1 set/family
socks, wool	8		1 pair/person
mess kit	8		1 item/person
sweater, wool	8		1 item/person
camp cook kit	8		1 item/family
towel	8		1 item/person
baby supplies, if needed	8		1 item/person
lamps and lamp oil	8		1 item/family
fire extinguisher, A-B-C type	8		1 item/family
newspapers	7		1 item/person
tissue	7		2 pack/family
buckets, plastic, with tight lids	7		1 item/family
30-hour candle	7		2 item/person
blanket	7		2 item/person
bulb, extra	6		1 item/person
garbage bags, plastic, ties, various	6		1 item/person
mask, dust or surgical	6		1 item/person
soap	6		1 bar/person

Table 6. Stash Item List (10 & above: Portable)

Item	I	Q	Need
kindling	6		1 box/family
light stick	6		1 item/person
binoculars	6		1 pair/person
rifle, if you plan to hunt	6		1 item/as needed
shotgun, if you plan to hunt	6		1 item/as needed
Medicine dropper	5		1 item/person
napkins	5		5 item/person
blades, razor	5		2 item/person
fishing line w/ hooks and sinkers	5		1 feet/family
soap, liquid detergent	5		1 bottle/family
wire saw	5		1 item/person
air mattress	5		1 item/person
pins, clothes	5		1 item/family
containers, Plastic storage	5		1 item/person
Chlorine bleach	5		1 item/person
long thermal underwear	5		1 item/person
key set, backup, with safety deposit key	5		1 item/person
propane fuel bottle	5		2 item/family
personal hygiene items	4		1 set/as needed
cards, playing	3		1 deck/family
pet supplies	3		1 set/as needed
book, local plant guide	3		1 book/family

Table 7. The Natural Remedy Kit in Your *Go Pack*: adjust as needed

Item	Qty	OK	Usage
Apis Mellifica (homeopathic)	1 vial/family		Use for bee and insect bites.
Arnica Montana (homeopathic)	1 vial/family		Use for muscle soreness and bruises. You can also choose a gel form to apply directly to the skin.

Table 7. The Natural Remedy Kit in Your *Go Pack*: adjust as needed

Item	Qty	OK	Usage
Calendula gel (tube)	1 tube/ family		Use for cuts, scrapes, burns and insect bites.
Echinacea (extract)	1 bottle/ family		A natural antiseptic (dilute with a little water to apply to skin). This can also be taken as an immune enhancer or if you get sick—1 dropperful 3 to 4 times/day.
Honey	1 plastic container/ family		Use as directed in Appendix I, Symptoms and Remedies, in several places. See page 78.
Phosphorus (homeopathic)	1 bottle/ family		For bleeding, or dizziness.
Salt, non-iodized	1 small container/ family		Use as directed in Symptoms and Remedies, in several places. See page 88.
Baking soda	1 small plastic container/ family		Use as directed in Appendix I, Symptoms and Remedies, page 80.
Veratrum Album (homeopathic)	1 vial/fam- ily		Use to stop diarrhea.

Table 8. What Else to Take Along

Item	Where to Find It

Table 8. What Else to Take Along

Item	Where to Find It

Table 9. Where to Meet in an Emergency

Condition	Where to Meet
Outside the home	
Outside the neighborhood	
Out of Town, North	
Out of Town, East	
Out of Town, South	
Out of Town, West	

Table 10. Evacuation Worksheet

	What To Do:
D	Measure Distance to Event, miles
E	Measure bearing of Event, degrees clockwise from north
W	Measure bearing of Wind, degrees clockwise from north
S	Subtract the smaller bearing from the larger bearing
Evacuate if S<15° and D is close enough to be dangerous	
V	Estimate speed of wind, mph
H	Divide D by V to get hours
T	Record the Time the event occurred
A	Add T to H and leave before this time:

Table 11. Friends' Skills and Resources

Name/Phone/Email	Skills & Resources

Table 12. FEMA Recommended Food Items

Item	Need	Notes
Wheat or other grain	20 lb/pers/mo	
Powdered infant formula	20 lb/pers/mo	in Nitrogen-packed cans
Corn	20 lb/pers/mo	
Iodized Salt	1 lb/pers/mo	
Soybeans	10 lb/pers/mo	
Vitamin C	15 gr/pers/mo	rotate at least every 2 years

Table 12. FEMA Recommended Food Items

Item	Need	Notes
Meat		canned ready to eat
Fruits		canned ready to eat
Vegetables		canned ready to eat
Juices, canned		
Milk, powdered		
Soup		
Sugar		
Vitamins		
Cereals		in plastic containers
Crackers, dry, crisp		in plastic containers
Potatoes		fresh or dried flakes
Foods, special		for elders or special diets
Vegetable oils		
Baking powder		
Beans, Rice		
Soft drinks		Noncarbonated
Bouillon products		
spices		
Dry pasta		
peanut butter, jelly		high energy
granola bars		high energy
trail mix		high energy
cookies		Comfort/stress foods
hard candy, lollipops		Comfort/stress foods
instant coffee, tea bags		Comfort/stress foods
cocoa, chocolate bars		Comfort/stress foods
canned nuts		Comfort/stress foods

Copy this blank list for other lists, like To-Do, What I Need, etc.

Table 13. Empty List

Item	Date	Quantity

Fold this page in half, toward binding, for security.

Table 14. Password Stash

Account	Username	P/W Hint

Bibliography

EVERYTHING YOU NEED TO KNOW, YOU LEARNED FROM NOAH'S ARK...
WHEN YOU SEE A PROBLEM, FIND A SOLUTION.

Angier, Bradford. *Staying Alive in the Woods.* Simon & Schuster, N.Y., 1983.

Bennett, Doug. *Life and Spirit in the Quantum Field: Spirit is Real, Feelings Rule, and other Adventures in Quantum Life.* Brevard, N.C.: Take Charge Books. 2012.

Bremness, Lesley. *Herbs.* Readers Digest Press, Pleasantville, N.Y., 1990.

Carr, Bernie. *The Prepper's Pocket Guide: 101 Easy Things You Can Do to Ready Your Home for a Disaster.* Berkeley, Calif: Ulysses Press. 2011.

Ceballos, Gerardo et al. "The Sixth Extinction Crisis: Loss of Animal Populations and Species," *Journal of Cosmology,* 2010, Vol 8, 1821-1831.

Churchill, James E. *Basic Essentials Survival.* The Globe Pequote Press, Guilford, Conn., 1999.

Crockett, Barry G., and Lynette B. Crockett. *72-Hour Family Emergency Preparedness Checklist.* Publishers Press, Salt Lake City, Ut., 1983.

Cummings, Stephen, M.D. and Dana Ullman. *Everybody's Guide to Homeopathic Medicines: Taking Care of Yourself and Your Family with Safe and Effective Remedies.* M.P.H. Putnam, N.Y., 1991.

Fischer, William L. *Miracle Healing Power Through Nature's Pharmacy.* Fischer Publishing Corp., Canfield, Oh., 1986.

Frist, William H. Sen. *When Every Moment Counts: What You Need to Know About Bioterrorism from the Senate's Only Doctor.* Rowman & Littlefield, 2002.

Gibbons, Euell. *Stalking the Healthful Herbs,* David McKay Co., N.Y. 1970.

Goll, John. *The Camper's Pocket Handbook,* The Globe Pequote Press, Guilford, Conn., 1992.

Heinerman, John. *Heinerman's New Encyclopedia of Fruits & Vegetables.* Prentice Hall, Paramus, N.J., 1995.

Hutchens, Alma R. *Indian Herbalogy of North America.* Shambhala, Boston, MA, 1991.

Kerr, Richard A. "Experts Agree Global Warming Is Melting the World Rapidly," *Science*, 30 November 2012: Vol. 338, no. 6111, p. 1138.

Kowalchik, Claire and William Hylton, eds. *Rodale's Illustrated Encyclopedia of Herbs.* Rodale Press, Emmaus, PA, 1987.

Lauck, Joanne Elizabeth. *The Voice of the Infinite in the Small*, Boston, Mass. Shambhala, 2002.

Lockie, Andrew and Dr. Nicola Geddes. *Homeopathy: The Principles and Practice of Treatment.* Dorling Kindersley, N.Y., 1995.

Lovelock, J.E. "Gaia as seen through the atmosphere." *Atmospheric Environment* 1967, Elsevier. 6 (8): 579–580.

O'Grady, Aingeal Rose. *A Time of Change.* Columbus, NC: Wild Flower Press, 2012.

Mabey, Richard. *The New Age Herbalist.* Simon & Schuster, N.Y.N.Y., 1988.

Schumacher, E. F. *Small Is Beautiful: A Study of Economics As If People Mattered* (1973, ISBN 0-06-131778-0)

Storey, John and Martha. *Basic Country Skills: A Practical Guide to Self-Reliance.* Storey Communications, Pownal, Vt., 1999.

Svensmark, Henrik and Nigel Calder. *The Chilling Stars: A Cosmic View of Climate Change.* Thriplow, Cambridge, England: Icon Books, Ltd. 2008.

Swedo, Suzanne. *Wilderness Survival.* Falcon Publishing, Helena, Mont., 1998.

Tawrell, Paul. *Camping & Wilderness Survival: The Ultimate Outdoors Book.* Paul Tawrell, Shelburne VT, 1996.

Theiss, Barbara & Peter. *The Family Herbal.* Healing Arts Press, Rochester, VT, 1989.

Waldman, Carl. *Atlas of the North American Indian.* Facts on File, Inc., 2009.

Weiss, Gaea and Shandor. *Growing & Using the Healing Herbs.* Rodale Press, Emmaus, Penn., 1985.

Wilson, Edward. O. *Biophilia.* Cambridge, Mass.: Harvard University Press, 1984.

Wiyaka, Gwilda. *So We're Still Here. Now What?: Spiritual Empowerment and Evolution in a New Era. Columbus, NC:* Swan-Raven & Co. 2012.

White, Linda B. & Foster, Steven. *The Herbal Drugstore.* Rodale, 2000.

Index

GRANITE PUBLISHING POB 1429 COLUMBUS NC 28722 828-894-8444		SOLID GROUND IN A SHIFTING WORLD	
WILD FLOWER PRESS:		DOCUMENTING THE UNEXPECTED	
A Time of Change: Akashic Guidance for Spiritual Transfor- mation	Aingeal Rose O'Grady		
SWAN-RAVEN & CO.:		ANCIENT WISDOM IN MODERN TIMES	
So, We're Still Here. Now What? Spiritual Evolution and Personal Empow- erment in a New Era	by Gwilda Wiyaka, Galactic Shamanism Practitioner		
NOT MADE BY HANDS.COM:		Cosmic Energy Essences	
Not Made By Hands: Energy Water from out of this world	Collected by Barbara Lamb Decoded by Aingeal Rose O'Grady via the Akashic Records		
GRANITE PUBLISHING:		HTTP://GRANITEPUBLISHING.US	
Common Sense in Uncommon Times: Survival in a Changing World	Brian L. Crissey and Pamela Meyer Crissey		
Online Access to All Tables in PDF format:		Join our mailing list for updates and more information:	